CSR History and Practice

AF192018

To Nina and Arthur

Knut-Erland Berglund

CSR HISTORY AND PRACTICE: A STUDY OF SWEDISH LARGE-SCALE ENTREPRENEURSHIP AT THE COMPANY LEVEL CIRCA 1940 – 2010

© 2025 Knut-Erland Berglund

Korrekturläsning: Nina Zebergs, Knut-Erland Berglund

Förlag: BoD · Books on Demand, Östermalmstorg 1, 114 42
Stockholm, Sverige, bod@bod.se
Tryck: Libri Plureos GmbH, Friedensallee 273, 22763 Hamburg,
Tyskland

ISBN: 978-91-8080-863-7

Preface

Already in the mid-2000s, I became interested in issues related to economic-political intersections, as I began to investigate microfinance in the then Indian state of Andhra Pradesh. Microfinance was large-scale when you looked at the number of practitioners in the state but small-scale in the microfinance bank with which I wrote a thesis. Microfinance is a form of socially and economically oriented savings groups that borrow from special microfinance banks, which provide relatively small loans. A loan cycle reviews the needs of local groups and anyone who wants to invest is vetted by other members of the group.

This type of strategy was seen, among other things, as a new form of input into the aid debate, that small loans from below would have a major impact on the borrowers and the greater economic development in developing countries. States were seen in these countries as less trustworthy due to corruption and powerlessness among citizens. Microfinance would help reduce poverty worldwide. This movement also has a normative content in terms of spreading knowledge about economics and savings to various formations of different groups such as the uncaste people in India.

When I later visited the Human Rights Days in Stockholm, a year later, I saw that the business community was there and discussing how companies could be a bridge between the state and society. This gave me an interest in human rights, the environment and social issues because it was on the agenda and "there and then". I came to investigate what this was more closely, and I began to realize what Corporate Social Responsibility (CSR) meant. I was then able to further my research within the framework of a doctoral program at Uppsala University and graduated with a licentiate degree in 2013.

Over the years, I had accumulated a large amount of material, empirical evidence, which I felt should not be discarded but used. With this, a few years later I began working on this script, which led to the production of this book. I think that over the course of the journey, it has become even more fun to deal with these issues, and I hope that you too will come to realize that CSR is important not only for the business community but for society as such. CSR may not be the whole solution to a more sustainable society, socially, economically or environmentally, but it is part of present and future business.

Uppsala May 2025

Knut-Erland Berglund,

Licentiate of Philosophy in Economic History,

Master of Philosophy in Economic History

Bachelor of Philosophy in Geography

Table of Contents

Introduction and background: Corporate Social Responsibility 9

Background to CSR 13

A Brief history of the companies 16

    The telephony company Ericsson 16

    The rubber company Trelleborg 18

    Hydropower company Vattenfall 19

CSR history and practice 21

Sponsorship of culture, sports and educational scholarships 21

    Ericsson 21

    Trelleborg 23

    Vattenfall 26

Corporate defense and Corporate fire brigade 28

    Ericsson 28

    Trelleborg 30

    Vattenfall 30

Corporate aid work and poverty alleviation 33

    Ericsson 33

    Trelleborg 37

    Vattenfall 38

Personnel policy 43

    Personnel policy - Shares 43

    Ericsson 43

    Trelleborg 43

    Personnel policy: Ceremonies in various forms 44

    Ericsson 44

    Trelleborg 45

I

Vattenfall..47

Personnel policy: Health-promoting strategies............................49

    Ericsson 49

    Trelleborg..51

    Vattenfall..54

Personnel policy: Gender equality, daycare and summer camp activities...56

    Ericsson 56

    Trelleborg..58

    Vattenfall..59

Personnel policy: Establishment of new communities...................61

    Vattenfall..61

Personnel policy: Corporate democracy and suggestion activities..62

    Trelleborg..62

    Vattenfall..63

Environmental work: From environmental price to energy saving......66

    Ericsson 66

    Trelleborg..69

    Vattenfall..72

Understanding the concept of CSR..76

    Ericsson, Trelleborg & Vattenfall..76

Analytical discussion 78

  Summary & comments 78

  Sponsorship of culture, sports and education 78

  Corporate security and corporate fire brigade 79

  Aid and poverty alleviation 80

  Personnel policy 83

  Environmental work 86

  The CSR concept..87

Sources and further reading.. 89

  Staff magazines: 89

  Further Reading: 89

Thanks! 91

Introduction and background: Corporate Social Responsibility

Corporate Social Responsibility (CSR) is a way for companies to relate to society and the stakeholders that surround the areas of business. This is according to the stakeholder model, which describes the actors who influence or are influenced by the company's activities. The areas of concern include the environment, human rights and personnel policy. This book attempts to situate the Swedish development of CSR practice and CSR history from a corporate and societal perspective.

Research and popular science publications have shown that activities that can be categorized as CSR have existed in a Scandinavian situation for over a hundred years, even though the concept itself came into being much later. The stakeholder model, which is a basis for understanding CSR where different interests have been balanced over time, is shown by researchers Ihlen & von Weltzien Hoivik to be valid even in a Scandinavian context. Companies have a history of CSR-like actions. This means that companies are driven by costs and profits but are just as much a social phenomenon as there are norms, behaviour and attitudes that are rewarded at different times.

One reason why CSR has been adopted by large companies (and at the time of writing by smaller companies and other organizations) is because of the prevailing economic policy ideas that flourished during the period under study (approximately 1940 to 2010). The fact that there are many large companies in Sweden is due to the economic rules that globalization has brought, where a tendency for capitalism is growth and the creation of ever larger organizations. There has also been a conscious policy during the 20th century, including by social democratic governments in collaboration with LO (the National Confederation of

Trade Unions). An example of this cooperation can be seen in the Rehn-Meidner model where policy would strengthen large companies in favour of small companies that would be rationalized away for more efficient companies.

Despite the existence of large companies, there has been scepticism among the social partners (SAF and LO) towards CSR, where CSR has been viewed with scepticism or perhaps even as a "cat among ermines" (hence, not as fancy). Nevertheless, it is a common phenomenon in Swedish business today, and there are large and small players who conduct, for example, personnel policies and environmental work with thoughts about a sustainable society.

Others, such as professor and ethicist Hans De Geer, emphasize that there is a social contract between politics and businesses about how economic and social policy should be carried out. Under *the Swedish model*, society was largely organized in such a way that social issues and the public sector were reserved for politics and companies were responsible for production issues where working conditions were negotiated with unions. The Swedish model has many definitions depending on what is intended. The Swedish model can be traced to the party relationships that were established between central organizations for employees (SAF) and employers (LO) and the outcome of these negotiations.

Under the Swedish model, the division between business, municipality and state is managed. The state would take care of welfare while companies transferred funds to it. Was this relationship so idealistic or what about CSR? Is there a history of CSR in Swedish companies?

With the development of financial markets, civil society and increasing globalization, this social contract looks different today. An important aspect is to discuss differences over time and between how the social contract is perceived and what is actually done by the business community. The Swedish model is an important part of the history of the policy pursued in the area but also of the economic reality. This book discusses the development of CSR and how a practice has emerged.

This book is preceded by the Licentiate thesis in economic history: *Corporate Social Responsibility rhetoric of large Swedish companies* by Knut-Erland Berglund from 2013. It studied the 50 largest companies in the Swedish economy based on the type of CSR communication they conducted during the period 1999 – 2010. This was a period when CSR and sustainability reports were initiated and popularized. The selection of companies to study the long-term development of CSR and CSR was based on the type of communication they conducted. As well as what potential there was for a longitudinal study regarding available archival material. The companies that were investigated and are being investigated in this book are Ericsson, Trelleborg and Vattenfall. The company magazines that were found in archived form or on special company websites contained different forms of internships and these were categorized and analysed.

Sweden is perceived as a socially oriented welfare country with capitalist characteristics. Sweden is an open market economy with large international trade, and this is reflected in the CSR work in the companies surveyed. The companies surveyed are, to borrow an English expression, "embedded" or permeated by society and vice versa. It turns out: in a pluralistic society, the state cannot do everything, but neither can companies.

With my book, I want to show that CSR cannot be overlooked in welfare Sweden, in a broad sense. Welfare is irreplaceable, but it is also work that is carried out by other actors over time. Like Swedish companies, through the Operational defense/Corporate defense, were part of the Home defense and thus the Total defense of Sweden during and after the Second World War. In question after question, Swedish companies are involved and take social responsibility in everything from aid, defense to gender equality. The Swedish model was thus more embedded in the companies' responsibility without jeopardizing what companies do best on the surface, which is to make a profit.

Background to CSR

The source that most people refer to when it comes to the historical development of CSR is Howard Bowen's *"Social Responsibility of the Businessman"* (1953), which is seen as the first work on CSR. From a Swedish perspective, researcher Eric Rhenman (1964) can also be counted among the first. It is probably the case that CSR practice itself is much older than that, as has been shown by Scandinavian and American researchers.

Researcher Bowen attempted to explain the obligations that businesspeople have towards society and how society's institutions can be transformed to support CSR work. The book was a success, and more and more organizations and companies came to strengthen employee protection and consumer rights. Even though corporate leaders officially advocated CSR, it was not certain that it would trickle down throughout the entire corporate structure because it was uncertain whether companies' CSR work could affect opportunities in the (financial) market. Something that was discussed further and is still discussed today.

The focus in the 1970s was on conceptualizing CSR. Researchers tried to study the practical work instead of discussing whether companies should have CSR at all. In practice, this meant that shareholders argued that if they invested in a diversified stock portfolio and ensured that monopolies were weakened, they would have fulfilled the requirement of "social responsibility", since the risks were spread. There was thus an emphasis on financial responsibility.

One of the most significant works written in the 1970s was by the researcher Carroll (1979), which contributed to the academic debate taking a leap forward in the 1980s. This contributed to developing CSR through CSP (Corporate Social Performance).

Unlike CSR, CSP can stem from the social issues that one works with and how these are relevant to the company in relation to the social issues that are of societal concern. CSP work thus involves the principles, processes and issues ("policies") that give CSR work meaning, according to researchers Wartick & Cochran. Despite these insights, companies did not adopt the CSP model because it was too theoretical.

The CSP model was further developed during the 1990s and enriched with institutional and stakeholder theories. Carroll's pyramid of CSR included financial, legal, ethical, and philanthropic practices. CSP became a large part of the companies' work on quality, customer satisfaction, and at the same time, new products were developed based on insights from these areas. Although CSR came to be linked to corporate success in general, large companies had some doubts about CSR's connection to financial profits.

During the 2000s, stakeholder theories were developed more extensively and contributed to the theoretical development of CSR by finding answers to questions about whether financial returns improve because of a company's CSR policy. Theorizing of this nature in turn assisted in attempts to measure the results of corporate sustainability work by studying specific stakeholders and not just shareholders. This opened new fields where CSR came to include inclusion, diversity, the environment and transparency in corruption issues. It is debatable whether CSR affects the financial market, and the issue was not resolved during the period.

An important distinction of CSR is between CSR as explicit versus implicit according to researchers Matten & Moon. This discussion indicates that it is relevant to discuss CSR as something that is done but also communicated. Where practice is more implicit and communication more explicit, but where the dividing line is can be very fine. Matten & Moon argued that there was a clear dividing line in the 2000s between the American and European experience regarding CSR, but that boundary is perhaps more theoretical than actual. It became apparent during the 2010s that more and more regions and countries are contributing to the development of the practice, and the concept means that there is a trend towards more and more countries adopting CSR as a practice and idea. Furthermore, there is research that shows that CSR has developed over time and that in some form the practice has existed for over a hundred years. This practice takes different forms in the countries where the concept has landed and/or if there has been practice that has been like CSR before the concept arrived.

A Brief history of the companies

The three companies whose communication and practices have been investigated also have a history behind them. What products have they created and what industry do they operate in? Have they grown internationally? An understanding of the companies is built up in order to be able to discuss and analyse them based on the companies' social responsibility.

The telephony company Ericsson

Ericsson's history, which has included products in telephony and telephone exchanges, began with Lars Magnus Ericsson establishing a mechanical workshop in Stockholm in 1876. Business grew and in 1896 the company was organized as a limited company; LM Ericsson & Co. Ericsson had an early internationalization process with markets in Norway, Denmark, Finland, Russia, Australia, New Zealand, the United Kingdom and China. This growth in international markets was due to the fact that fierce competition at home pushed Ericsson out into the international market, in order to survive as a company. From the early 20th century, markets in Great Britain, Mexico and Austria-Hungary also increased.

In 1918, Ericsson merged with Stockholms Allmänna Telefon AB, another telephone company, because they could achieve economies of scale with the merger. However, the Krueger crash also affected Ericsson. Kreuger owned a considerable share of shares in Ericsson and with Kruger's death, a game about Ericsson began to unfold. This gamble resulted in the two banks with strong shares, Svenska Handelsbanken and Stockholm's Enskilda Bank, taking over control of Ericsson.

During the 1940s, Ericsson moved to its premises in Midsommarkransen, approximately 5 kilometres from Stockholm. The Second World War disrupted contact with international markets, however, military buildup opened new markets for Ericsson. After 1945, the company expanded its business internationally with products such as the coordinator changer. Mexico and Brazil became important markets. Ericsson was established shortly after World War II in Denmark, Norway, Finland, the Netherlands, France, Great Britain, Spain and Italy.

Production also expanded in Sweden after the war, and Ericsson production units were established in most small towns and cities. The close connection between the military was maintained between 1960 and 1990 when, for example, Ericsson developed an airborne radar in close collaboration with SAAB. The AXE system, the new coordinator exchange system, was also a success story during the period. The period 1977–1990 was a time when new mobile technology was rapidly developed by Ericsson. Mobile phones were for a time one of the most significant markets for the company, along with the coordinator switching system. From the 1990s onwards, it was the new organizational form of "outsourcing" that also became important for Ericsson in a global world. Outsourcing means that production units were moved to areas with lower production costs.

In 2001, Ericsson celebrated its 125th anniversary with festive publications and pomp and show. The company used its role in Swedish history to highlight a proud tradition and history. Even during the 2000s, Ericsson was an important player in its industry, in business and for Swedish society, even though production decreased in Sweden.

The rubber company Trelleborg

The company was established in 1905 and specialized in producing rubber products such as tires and raincoats. A merger between the companies of Johan Kock and Henry Duncker established the base for Trelleborg in 1905. The First World War had a positive impact on the company, as profits almost doubled due to inflation and the company made successful product innovations. The poor supply of raw rubber forced the company to be innovative by using chemicals from used rubber products.

The interwar years were associated with both decline and rise in business volumes. The year 1926 marked the beginning of an internationalization phase when Trelleborg established itself in the United Kingdom. During World War II, the supply of raw rubber was limited, which meant that Trelleborg was forced to increase efficiency, once again, in production.

During the 1950s and 1960s, demand for Trelleborg's products increased due to the increased use of cars and trucks, which needed rubber products such as tires. Demand from the Swedish defense also increased during the Cold War. In the 1950s, Trelleborg internationalized on a full scale. A network of agents and dealers was established in 65 countries. It took some time before the first factory was established and it was in Holland in 1962. Trelleborg also grew in Sweden during the period through company acquisitions.

In 1975, the golden era of the Swedish economy was over, and the production of rubber products decreased due to the aftermath of the oil crisis (1973). The result for Trelleborg was to achieve a lean organization, where Trelleborg ended its production of rubber tires and almost all production of bicycle tires. However, Trelleborg began to expand in its markets during the 1980s, following a radical restructuring and a strong capital rationalization program. In 1986, Trelleborg acquired the much larger company Boliden AB to expand a conglomerate.

A brief crisis occurred when metal prices fell in 1991, which required a restructuring of the company to strengthen business. During the 2000s, Trelleborg concentrated and cultivated its focus on heavy industry through the acquisition of three English companies: Invensys, Smiths Group Plc and Polymer Sealing Solutions.

Hydropower company Vattenfall

Vattenfall began its activities in 1909 when the Swedish state decided to actively develop the electricity market. This decision resulted, among other things, in the construction of the Trollhätte Canal. In the early 1910s, the Porjus and Älvkarleby power stations were also built, which were significant projects for the time. The expansion of the power grid continued during the 1920s with the interconnection of distribution and transformer stations.

The 1940s and 1950s were characterized by a time when hydropower was developed and technology advanced. The Second World War had an impact on how hydroelectric power was built because Sweden was cut off from the international energy market. Coal in particular became subject to rationalization and Sweden was forced to rely on hydropower. During the 1940s and 1950s, the big leap came when the development of the northern rivers was linked to the cities in the south through electric power. During the 1960s, the expansion of hydroelectric power in the northern rivers continued. During this period, nuclear power also came to play a greater role. During the 1970s, public environmental interest began to influence Vattenfall's activities, particularly in matters relating to nuclear power.

During the liberalization of markets in the 1990s, Swedish politicians incorporated Vattenfall and a limited company was formed in 1992. According to Carl Erik Nyqvist, the corporate culture was also transformed during the incorporation, where the company came to adopt a stakeholder analysis of its relationships with the surrounding society. Vattenfall also wanted to change its media image from being a bureaucratic colossus to a modern company, which also changed their external communication. An internationalization phase began in the 1990s, when Vattenfall was first established in the Nordic markets. Vattenfall continued its expansion into countries such as Germany, Poland and the Far East. The parliamentary decision to phase out nuclear power had a major impact on Vattenfall, which came to develop more environmentally friendly electricity such as bioenergy, electric cars and so on. However, the acquisitions of nuclear power plants in Germany demonstrated Vattenfall's continued tradition in the area.

CSR history and practice

Practice during the period 1940 to 2010 shows that large Swedish companies were early involved in issues that today can be understood as CSR practice. CSR practice and CSR commitment involved categories such as: *Sponsorship of culture, sports and education, company security and company fire brigades, aid and poverty alleviation, personnel policy (shares, ceremonies, health promotion strategies, gender equality, daycare and colony activities, establishment of new communities and company democracy and suggestion activities), environmental issues and the understanding of the CSR concept.* These categories were an analytical result of the work with the archival material.

Sponsorship of culture, sports and educational scholarships

Culture, sports and sponsorship were a central part of corporate engagement for the period under review. In recent decades, these commitments have generated cultural sponsorship for scholarships for students and were a recurring theme throughout the period. Ericsson was the company whose sponsorship decreased over time; however, activities were greater in Trelleborg and Vattenfall.

Ericsson

Travel grants were established during the 1940s for further education and research grants for those within Ericsson who wanted to pursue a doctorate. A library was established in 1941, and the following year books were donated to the library by employees. A modest library existed as early as 1935. A common room was also built for the employees of Midsommarkransen.

Ericsson also sponsored scholarships for exchanges to the United States and other travel grants during the 1950s. During the next decade, the 1950s, Ericsson sponsored and opened a museum in Värmskog, Värmland about the founder Lars Magnus Ericsson. This was Lars Magnus' birthplace. The museum was the result of a collaboration with local heritage organizations and the company.

Most of the buildings were constructed to meet the needs of the employees during the 1960s. In 1961, the library was one of the largest corporate libraries in Sweden with over 30,000 volumes. The library had expanded during the 1950s and 1960s as technological advances brought with them an increased amount of literature. Another initiative by LM Ericsson was Midsommargården, which was intended to be an alternative to youth camps, combining play and fun with education. There, several generations could gather and study courses such as Bible studies, astronomy, classical dance and radio telegraphy. In 1961, approximately 1,200 young people studied there, led by about 20 teachers. Even during the 1960s, scholarships were awarded to employees who wanted to travel to learn a new language, new technical skills, or who wanted to study at a Swedish or international university.

There was also access to educational scholarships for Ericsson employees during the 1970s and 1980s. In 1995, the scholarship program funded a doctoral student at Uppsala University who was focused on engineering physics at the Kaj Siegbahn laboratory.

In the period 2000 to 2010, social sponsorship increased in Ericsson, where the Botkyrka Project was launched in 2006, together with the Confederation of Swedish Enterprise and Botkyrka Municipality. This project would increase integration into society and provide the company with employees with language and technical qualifications from several other countries. Botkyrka is a municipality where many new Swedes and those who have previously immigrated have established themselves.

Trelleborg

During the 1940s, the Trelleborg company sponsored motorsports such as Formula 1 with tires and other equipment. When it comes to sponsoring sports, Trelleborg sponsored motorsport during the decade as a motorcycle racer, led by world champion Lasse Gustavsson. Even "Within the Walls," the Trelleborg company ensured that employees had access to tennis, bowling, archery and handball to stay in shape.

One of the more spectacular events that Trelleborg was involved in and supported financially was the salvage in 1957 of the 17th-century ship Vasa. Trelleborg, which had extensive knowledge in the rubber field, contributed with specially made rubber products that enabled the salvage of the ship. It involved diving suits, various ventilation systems and hoses, as well as large-format inflatable rubber balloons to ensure the rescue was successful. A group of companies and the Swedish King Carl XIV Gustav contributed to the salvage of Vasa due to the Swedish state's failure to provide funds. This initiative resulted in a museum in the capital, Stockholm, which is widely known and visited.

In 1958, 235 vacation allowances were awarded to everyone who had at least 10 years of employment. In 1956, a scholarship was also awarded from Trelleborgs Gummifabriks Aktiebolag's fiftieth anniversary fund, which was the company's anniversary gift to the educational institution and was awarded to Lars Göran A. Nilsson. After being awarded the scholarship, the then 18-year-old Lars Göran devoted himself to technical studies at Chalmers. In previous summers, he had also interned at Trelleborg's construction office. During the 1950s, Trelleborg's staff magazine (T-nabben) had a cottage at Maglasäte in Skåne that employees could use. The orienteering club had primarily used this facility. The cottage was located close to nature, and it was also possible to use the sauna!

When it comes to personnel policy, there are several different elements as follows: Trelleborg offered free training for office staff in Swedish and mathematics. Company knowledge was also on the agenda. There were also plans to offer training courses to learn how to handle books in a systematic way.

During the 1960s, interest in Trelleborg increased for employees to get involved in sporting activities such as archery, bandy, bowling, golf, ice hockey, swimming, tennis and athletics. These activities arose from the company doctor's initiative to improve the health of employees. An active lifestyle was considered important, and several sports facilities were established.

The company newspaper (T-blandning) had a holiday cottage, which burned down in 1969, this one in Ljungby. At midsummer 1965, the Greek club at Trelleborg had a free outing for employees. 273 people at the Trelleborg Group received holiday allowances from the Henry Dunker holiday foundation and each person received 100 SEK. They had to have been employed for ten years to receive the grant in 1965. A total of 24.300 kronor was distributed from Henry Dunker's holiday foundation, each in 100 kronor increments, in 1961.

At the graduation ceremony of Söderslätt's Upper secondary school in Trelleborg, the largest financial scholarship in the school's history was awarded. It was 2.950 kronor from Trelleborg's 50 year-fund. Engineer Curt Bergling was awarded 9.350 kronor for design proposals that radically simplified and reduced the cost of manufacturing certain meld tools. Since 1963, proposals have been rewarded with a total sum of SEK 120.000 from the Trelleborg Group. An increased contribution to employees taking correspondence courses was provided by Trelleborg. Scholarships for technical evening school were given to those who graduated from this technical education, of 250 and 150 kronor respectively. Scholarships were awarded to those who had studied in evening school and these were rewarded with 15 vacation trips to Italy for 8 days in 1963. Scholarships were given to high school students to attend technical conferences in 1960 and 1962. The proposal activity to improve production was rewarded with 5.000 kronor and a trip to North America in 1960.

In the 1970s, Trelleborg continued to support motorsport, including rally drivers Eva Andersson and Rose-Marie Strand, as well as Jens Nielsen in the Monte Carlo Rally. They sponsored with winter friction tires. A project was also sponsored to reduce sports injuries, using Trelleborg's special rubber and plastic flooring.

Regarding scholarships, Sven Andersson and Kenneth M Persson each received a Berzelius scholarship in 1983. From Trelleborgs AB's 59th anniversary fund, two scholarships of SEK 4.000 each were awarded to two high school students in Trelleborg. Berzelius scholarships were also awarded in 1985 and 1986. In 1988, seven scholarships were awarded to high school students in Trelleborg totalling 41.500 kronor. Scholarships rained down on students when 89,000 kronor was awarded to 20 students at Söderslätt's Upper secondary school in Trelleborg in 1994. Also in 1995, approximately 50.000 SEK was distributed to students at Söderslätt's Upper secondary school from Trelleborg AB's 50th anniversary fund. Also in 1996, approximately 60.000 SEK was awarded to the graduating class in Trelleborg.

At the beginning of 1982, an art association was opened in Trelleborg to ensure that art took hold in the company. This was more locally anchored to the head office and the municipality of Trelleborg. Interest in art increased during the 1980s and two years later the association had over 400 members. In addition to art, the Trelleborg company also had a prominent sports club in the 1980s, in everything from badminton to shooting and tennis. Trelleborg continued to sponsor motorsport as

Sweden's contribution to the 1984 World Enduro Championships, but also in 1988 it sponsored motocross with rubber tires from Trelleborg. The year before, an expedition to Mount Everest had also caught the company's interest. Tents and other equipment were provided to the group that climbed the world's highest mountain so that they could cope with the specific and harsh conditions that prevail there.

In Trelleborg, sports continued to be an important part of the staff's health work during the 1990s, with aerobics sometimes being given every Tuesday to interested employees. Trelleborg continued its involvement in motorsport and sponsored Formula 1.

Vattenfall

During the 1940s, Vattenfall opened sports clubs in Motala (1949) which were planned for office staff so that they could train their bodies in aerobics, among other things.

It was true that an active sports culture flourished at Vattenfall during the 1950s. In 1952, the company established an organization for all sports in the company to coordinate activities and exchanges between locations within the corporate group. The organization supported football, orienteering, shooting, slalom, swimming and table tennis tournaments. In 1953, Vattenfall established a photography club to organize competitions in photography of landscapes and company activities such as sports.

During the 1960s, Vattenfall arranged a campaign to attract employees to physical activity with Roland Hammarström's campaign "Flex with Roland". Roland was described as a jovial director who would get many people moving during working hours. The cultural side of Vattenfall's corporate activities also sponsored activities at the Royal Dramatic Theatre, popularly known as "Dramaten" during this period.

Vattenfall's headquarters in Råcksta housed Dr. Stig Valentin, who during the 1970s discussed in the company magazine how sports and recreation could improve the health of employees, after which 500.000 SEK was invested in sports activities such as badminton, bowling, ice hockey, skiing and table tennis. A gym break with short exercises (about 5 minutes) was introduced during the period for better health in the company. There were also specific activities for women such as orienteering and tennis. The cultural vein was also maintained with the establishment of a national art association with its first annual meeting in May 1977.

Vattenfall invested in eleven postgraduate training positions and a professorship at the Royal Institute of Technology (KTH). Chalmers in Gothenburg also received funding from the company to establish young researchers as lecturers during the period 1984 to 1987. During the 1980s, Vattenfall had a shooting organization, and this tournament recurred annually during the period. Approximately SEK 100.000 went to the company's sports section for maintenance and fees. Vattenfall also sponsored women's motorsport in 1989. A committee was appointed in Vattenfall to cultivate history in the company and this conservation committee gave artifacts to the Technical Museum in Stockholm, namely turbine blades from the Lilla Edet hydroelectric power plant. This committee worked with historical materials, including from the company's history.

At Vattenfall, cultural activities were underway and "Othello" at the Stockholm Opera House was sponsored together with several other companies. In addition, Vattenfall established an opera academy for education and the motto is to create a creative culture and business climate in Sweden and abroad. Vattenfall continued to sponsor opera and culture with a festival at Savolinna Palace in Helsinki in 2000.

Corporate defense and Corporate fire brigade

During the 1940s, a military organization was established in companies, which I have chosen to call corporate defense since these were at the company level. These were called Operational guards. This applied to Ericsson, Trelleborg and Vattenfall until the 1980s/1990s. The Corporate defense was part of the Home Guard, which meant that the companies that organized themselves provided the Home Guard with equipment after specialization, and that defense exercises were conducted during working hours. The Corporate defense was also part of the Total defense and cooperated on several levels. The Home Guard was a spontaneous movement during the occupations that took place in neighbouring countries during World War II and was regulated by national legislation. There was also a fire department in the companies that would cooperate with the police, primarily but also society at large, in disaster situations.

Ericsson

During the 1940s, the Ericsson company paid approximately SEK 350,000 for defense material for the group at the price level of the time through donations in 1941 and 1942. This corresponds to approximately 9 million SEK in today's value. It was considered very serious to be part of the company security force, as it was described in Ericsson's company magazine from the 1940s that a "soldier" would always be on his toes if something happened. Otherwise, he would do field exercises and practice shooting. For example, one autumn day in 1941, attack exercises against Älvsjö were held for a whole day.

The Swedish Lotta Corps, which assisted the Home Guard, was also there and served pasta, sausages and soup. There was a division by gender, with men serving in the Home Guard and women in the Lotta

Corps. The Corporate's defense force was out in the field and spent the night to simulate the defense of the factories in wartime. It was proclaimed in Ericsson's company newspaper by the Executive Vice President (CEO) that it was of utmost importance and in the national interest to participate in the defense. It was also generally seen as an important part of occupational health to practice occupational safety. There were also occasions when Ericsson's defense forces took part in the High Guard at Stockholm Castle, when 22 employees participated in the High Guard on September 25–26, 1943. The organization also expanded after World War II.

During the 1950s, combat exercises continued because, even though World War II had ended, the atmosphere of the Cold War was affecting, which meant that there were risks in the world for new conflicts. Therefore, it was practiced in Ericsson's corporate defense during the period. The Corporate Guard celebrated its 10th anniversary in 1950, and a recurring ceremony was to give medals to the Lotta corps and home guards for their time and mission. There were 110 soldiers in Ericsson. In Ericsson, as in Trelleborg, the fire department overlapped with the company security. However, a fire department was not established in Ericsson until 1957. In 1962, military exercises continued in the Stockholm archipelago, for Ericsson.

During the 1970s, exercises continued in Ericsson in the Värmdö archipelago. Trelleborg's corporate security force consisted of 50 people trained in various skills in 1970. During this decade, the company fire department was dismantled, or rather, incorporated entirely into the municipal fire department.

During the 1980s, the corporate security at Ericsson celebrated its 40th anniversary. Otherwise, the reporting of the company security services sounded like something that would indicate that these were gradually being dismantled and dismantled.

Trelleborg

The Trelleborg fire department, or popularly known as "Fire-Johan", expanded in 1939 and became part of the municipal fire department in the same year. This was due to the additional legislation regulating the defense of airspace. The purpose of the company fire department was to assist the municipal fire department in the event of major accidents and disasters. Trelleborg made sure to modernize its fire department with water sprinklers, fire alarms and new concrete floors.

The Trelleborg company conducted grenade firing, machine gun shooting and distance measurement in two major exercises in 1964 and 1966. Interestingly, Trelleborg was involved in the development of the m/68, a so-called shoot-and-throw weapon, with the Swedish national defense in 1968. This indicates that the companies collaborated in different ways and levels in total defense, which included corporate and homeland defense. Trelleborg also collaborated with the police in the production of a protective vest that would withstand machine gun fire. In 1965, the 25th anniversary of Trelleborg's company security was celebrated and nine veterans received medals. In Trelleborg, shooting activities continued during the 1980s.

Vattenfall

R. Wanberg, who was Vattenfall's Industrial safety manager, made sure to win the national company competition in 1941. The Corporate guard participated in the exercises in Motala with grenade throwing, shooting and orientation near the Malfors regiment during the same year. In 1949, twenty employees from Vattenfall were sent to Jämtland to practice skiing, handling automatic weapons and other equipment. During the same year, machine gun shooting training was held in Motala. Later in the year, even larger exercises were held in the Västerås area where the then modern walkie-talkies were used for radio communication between different units.

In Vattenfall, a fire department had been established in 1951, and 16 men were recruited to handle this duty. In Vattenfall, the company security department was responsible for rebuilding the energy network in the event of sabotage by a foreign power. The Corporate Guard celebrated 10 years in 1951 at Vattenfall. Vattenfall's organization in Motala and Västerås continued to practice throughout the 1950s to maintain its knowledge of war situations. This organization also participated in the national tournament where the battalion from Västerås won in Stockholm in 1954. The fire department was established at Vattenfall to be able to handle risks and accidents in energy delivery and at the same time they could assist the municipal fire department if needed. This organization had a training base in Sundsvall where you could take courses and practice in fire protection.

Vattenfall's Corporate Guard participated in the Borga mountain exercises in 1957 and 1958, where the exercises were intended to provide knowledge about the highland conditions in the area. That same year, they were allowed to participate in the high guard at Stockholm Castle, the same as their counterparts at the Ericsson company. The following year, a corresponding unit from Norway, Vest-Opland, was in Trollhättan to train with Vattenfall's military organization. Also, that same year, exercises and competitions took place in Hammarforsen.

During the period, Vattenfall held an exercise where four hundred air troops practiced in Västerås. There was also cooperation with the National defense, where it was discussed what obligations, the company would have during wartime and how to prepare for this during peacetime in terms of the national energy supply. Even during the 1960s, the company security forces had exercises with maps, orientation, shooting, grenade throwing and mine-clearing. Vattenfall celebrated the 40th anniversary of its military organization in 1965. This was celebrated with an exercise outside Karlstad where a group from Berg won the competition. In 1968, military training was carried out in highland and inaccessible areas in Sweden. Vattenfall also had a fire department, including in Uppsala.

Exercises and competitions continued to be held at Vattenfall. In a competition outside Uppsala in Skogstibble, the Swedish guard won over the guards of other Nordic neighbours in 1978. The following year, the company security service was also opened to women as soldiers, with 21 women participating in training and exercises in Råcksta and Vällinge. Among other things, shooting with the Carl Gustav M/45 submachine gun was on the schedule. Vattenfall's fire department was part of the municipal fire department during the period. Vattenfall also conducted exercises in Vadstena in 1988.

Corporate aid work and poverty alleviation

The studied Swedish corporations have contributed to poverty alleviation in different forms. Certain institutionalisation by Ericsson was organised as a „Response" to contemporary issues. War times had effect upon what kind of relief that occurred.

Ericsson

Ericsson began donating clothing and money to our Nordic neighbours during World War II and shortly after the end of the war in the 1940s. The workers' union at Ericsson donated money to a fund for homeless children in Norway. Otherwise, the company gave a gift of freedom and peace to Norway in 1945. After the war, the work of rebuilding Europe and European Aid were supported, among other things, with a donation to Poland of 10,000 SEK in value at the time, as well as clothing for those in need.

The 1950s saw increased activity in the company with various stakeholders. Ericsson distributed funds for the construction of houses in the Po Valley, approximately one million lire in 1951. Two years later, the Netherlands received support after a storm with 65,000 SEK in then-current value when both the company and the employees jointly assisted. This aid was paid to the International Red Cross, which ensured that the money was converted into support and assistance. Hungary received a solidarity gift due to the Soviet Union's aggression against the popular uprising in 1956. This was based on a gift consisting of hours of work given up in exchange for money for Hungary. In Cali, Colombia, Ericsson used its know-how by replacing parts of the telecommunications system after a major earthquake in the same year as the Hungarian Uprising. The then President of Colombia, Gustovas Rojas Pinilla, expressed great gratitude to the company for their help.

During the 1960s, aid to Sweden was focused on the company and children with leprosy received a donation of 32,000 SEK. Ericsson employees also donated blood, ten thousand liters to the healthcare system. This donation began in the 1940s and was then sporadic but became increasingly organized during the 1960s.

An important part of the 1970s activities regarding development work at Ericsson was the establishment of *the LM-arnas Utlandsförening* (LMU) in 1976, LM after Lars Magnus Ericsson – the company's founder. They had an ambition to contribute to poverty alleviation and equalizing conditions for industrialized and developing countries. This organization in the company was inspired by the Swedish government's development assistance and poverty reduction agency, SIDA. The association's main goal was to show solidarity and to ensure that employees and more and more affected people would understand the situation in developing countries so that action could take place. LMU collaborated with various NGOs (non-governmental organizations) such as Amnesty International, Lutheran World Aid and Save the Children. LMU worked on four projects during the 1970s. These included support for the construction of a new mill for Brazilian farmers, a leprosy hospital in northern Yemen, food supplies and medicine for southern Yemen, and school donations to what was then Rhodesia and today's Zimbabwe. Thailand also received assistance from the company after the 1979 floods that affected 100.000 people. The employees in Bangkok collected and distributed clothes, matches, medicine, salt and money to those affected.

Another important organization for the company in aid matters was the establishment of *the International Telecommunications School* in 1977, which became an alternative to LMU. The stakeholders who were driving the school were Ericsson's own training institute, Telia (then the Swedish Televerket) and the company Swedtel, who designed the education according to international standards to find talent in all corners of the world.

During the 1980s, more specifically in 1981, LMU was closed due to internal disputes over the forms of aid. Interest in aid issues had decreased in Ericsson and the association lost momentum and members.

During the 1990s, unrest in the former Yugoslavia was on the agenda, and in Sarajevo, Ericsson rebuilt the telecommunications network in Sarajevo after a bomb attack on the city. In 1997, materials such as clothes and toys were given to orphans in a school in Romania. On the telecommunications track, the company invested in a master's degree program for Chinese students in Beijing. This training received around 30 students each year who would become future leaders in the industry and this was the first foreign training program established in the country by a company. As part of the China initiative, Ericsson donated GSM technology to the flooded areas of Helionjiang, Hubei and Jiangxi in 1998. This was a collaboration with the Red Cross and included 20 million kronor in value at the time. In Canada, a gala was organized to raise money for the homeless in Montreal. In Albania, telephone networks were donated and installed for refugees to call relatives back home.

A central part of its work on CSR was that in 1999 the company established a group to work on CSR. Pretty soon, the group developed into an institutionalized player within the company, collaborating with the Swedish Cancer Society, the World Childhood Foundation, and the International Red Cross.

In the 2000s, Ericsson launched a modern aid and poverty alleviation program and unit within the company called *Ericsson Response*. This entity signed an agreement with the United Nations (UN) to supply telecommunications equipment to the UN offices and headquarters in Brindisi - *United Nations Office for the Coordination of Humanitarian*

Affairs. This equipment would be used in disasters and other serious situations globally.

Ericsson Response donated mobile phones to storm victims via the Red Cross and its sister organization the Red Crescent, but also to areas such as Angola, Bosnia, East Timor, Congo and Sierra Leone. When terrorist attacks hit New York, among others, on September 11, 2001, Ericsson created software to find people under the rubble. Ericsson also helped increase the bandwidth and capacity of the telephone network during the period so that people could reach their loved ones. This was done by installing several antennas in the area. In addition, approximately 15 million SEK in then-current value was donated to families affected by the events of September 11. This was done via the Red Cross.

Ericsson Canada donated 400 mobile phones to people living under threat of violence. The phones were programmed to reach the emergency number 911 with the press of a button. In the same year, approximately SEK 27.000 in then-current value was given to refugees from Afghanistan. Ericsson Response and the Red Cross ensured that approximately 100.000 refugees in three camps had access to telecommunications in northwestern Tanzania. This was through GSM technology and stations. In 2002, a historic contract was made with the Red Cross, documenting and implementing the sharing of knowledge and personnel between these organizations in disaster situations.

In the aftermath of Hurricane Katrina in Florida, Ericsson Response aided with food, basic housing and water, as well as rebuilding the telecommunications network after this powerful and one of the worst disasters to hit the southwestern United States in 2005. That same year in Pakistan, Ericsson helped after the massive and powerful earthquake that killed more than 30.000 people. They helped with their industry knowledge and cooperation with the Red Cross by sending mobile phones and sending volunteers who could assist. El Salvador and Guatemala also received assistance after the floods in October 2005.

Another of the catastrophic events that hit the world was the 2004/2005 Tsunami, after which Ericsson Response was on site. They helped survivors make free calls from the local operator AIS in Thailand to several countries. Ericsson also rebuilt telecommunications in the Aceh province and Sri Lanka, which are vital in a society and especially in disaster situations. Approximately SEK 900.000 was also collected and donated to victims of the Tsunami. The following year, Ericsson Response was in Kashmir, India after an earthquake in the area and contributed its know-how.

Trelleborg

Trelleborg, the rubber and tire company, carried out the media-noticed "Operation Ice" in 1959, where three tons of ice, medicines and tires worth SEK 75.000 in then-current value were shipped from the Arctic Circle to countries around the African equator. Similar to Ericsson, blood was donated to the Swedish National Blood Service during the 1960s, 1961 and 1965, approximately 20.000 litres at a time were donated to, among other places, Lund in Skåne.

In 1963, the company's staff magazine (T-blending) was used to encourage employees to contribute to the Red Cross' national fundraiser. The purpose of this fund was to collect food, furniture, household appliances and medicines for an orphans' home. This focus on doing good took an international turn the following year when several countries received assistance from Trelleborg via the Red Cross in the form of clothing, food and medical care. Other more focused projects went to Italy due to child poverty and families without the means to support themselves because the adults were unemployed. Families in South Korea received assistance with funds for children in Kaesong

Pusan, for children and orphans' homes in Nea Makri, Athens, and for Hungarian refugees continued into the 1960s.

Trelleborg donated pens via Radiohjälpen, a NGO, to earthquake victims in Agdair, Morocco. In 1966, 20.000 SEK was donated by employees to a project to treat and reduce the suffering of cancer patients. Added to this was SEK 25.000 from the Henry and Gerda Dunkers Foundation, the owners of Trelleborg. There was no information about aid during the 1970s.

In 1982, Trelleborg supported hospitals, nursing homes and orphan homes around Szczecin in Poland. Approximately 150 tons or a value of 1.5 million kronor were shipped from Sweden in the form of food, hygiene products and shoes. The following year, Trelleborg supported the Save the Children organization by providing funds for drought-stricken areas in central and southern Africa. The projects where various orphanages were supported also continued during the 1980s.

Trelleborg's aid work during the 1990s sought to support various areas in Kazakhstan with equipment to protect themselves against oil and gas leaks. This included fire safety training at Victoria Fire Station in Uppsala worth 80.000 US dollars. In 1995, families employed at the factory in Sri Lanka were supported by providing glasses to everyone in need, and their children received schoolbooks and breakfast at school. Later, in 2005, Trelleborg provided financial support to rebuild a fishing village in Matara, Sri Lanka. In 2007, the collaboration with Save the Children was officially established.

Vattenfall

Kvinnor i Vattenfall (KIV) was formed in 1929 as The Swedish Water Authority's Women's Civil Servants' Association, the Swedish Water

Authority's Women's Association VKF. Until 1942, the chairman was "Mrs" Edith Lindberg. By 1963 it had been completely replaced by the association KIV, a section within the Swedish Vattenfall Corporation's Employees' Union, and in 1977 had about 200 members. The association was to benefit the interests of the female members, and the association was a way to strengthen solidarity between women. An example of this was when the association put pressure on the director general regarding salary grades for female civil servants (in 1930). KIV produced an information poster about the "Developing Country Woman" which was intended to talk about the situation of women in India (1989). This is in collaboration with the association Women in Time and SIDA. Money also went to strengthen women's educational situation in India.

Thirty-three Hungarian refugees landed in Sweden in 1956 and Vattenfall helped them find jobs and somewhere to live. KIV organized and collected clothes, household appliances, cutlery and toys for these refugees to be able to get their lives in order in the new country. This action was due to the Soviet intervention in 1956 in Hungary. Among the refugees who came to Bergeforsen in Sweden, a town built by Vattenfall to supply hydroelectric power to Swedish society. KIV also collected 56,000 SEK via the Red Cross and the City Mission in Sweden. The surplus from the Children's Collection was donated to a relief fund for refugee children for future needs. Approximately 20.000 kronor was donated to Save the Children and the Red Cross in 1958.

Since the late 1950s, Vattenfall has helped the Swedish Institute procure such electrical equipment for Pakistan and Ethiopia. Some provinces such as East Pakistan lacked electricity, telephones and radios, which Vattenfall supplied. Vattenfall was involved in moving the three-thousand-year-old Ramses statue on behalf of UNESCO, where other companies were also involved in the work. This is because the damming of the Nile could otherwise affect the statue. In 1966, 10.000 kronor went to the Cancer Fund.

About ten Vattenfall experts worked for SIDA for a time to organize and manage operation and maintenance at the Kafue Gorge Hydro Electric Scheme in Zambia. One of their main tasks for the aid was to train Zambians to operate a hydroelectric power plant themselves. The Swedes also brought clothing (335kg) to the population to assist them. The collaboration between SIDA and Vattenfall continued in 1974, with several people, including Bengt Mårtensson, traveling to Kenya in SIDA's service. This is to build power lines over a two-year period. The collaboration with SIDA also extended to Sri Lanka, where Vattenfall workers helped build hydroelectric power plants in 1979.

In 1980, personnel from Vattenfall worked for two years on a project in Mozambique for Swedpower, which had been commissioned by SIDA to conduct studies on the local power system. Swedpower is a subsidiary for foreign countries that offers consulting and expert assistance to power companies in other countries. Swedpower's mission includes checking and approving all technical specifications and drawings, as well as checking that work is being done in Mozambique. Swedpower signed a contract with Electricidade de Moçambique regarding consulting services for a power transmission project in the southern part of the country. Twenty-five technicians from 17 developing countries received nine weeks of training on international hydropower in Sweden during the 1980s. It was Vattenfall and Swedpower who organized the course at Häringe Castle outside Västerhaninge. Participants come from Papua New Guinea, China, the Dominican Republic and Ecuador, among others. It was debated in Vi Vattenfall whether Swedish industry had a good starting position regarding the electrification of developing countries and whether it could capitalize on this. This means that there was an underlying profit motive with the aid.

The business had been in operation for ten years in 1985 and had a turnover of 50 million SEK per year. The assistance has been in the form of expansion of local electricity systems with mini-power or expansion of remotely located larger power plants with transmission networks to urban centres or interconnection of national electricity systems. In all of these areas, Vattenfall has knowledge in the form of experienced technicians and planning systems. Often, developing country industry is relatively outdated and based on processes with high energy consumption. Training for developing countries – Twenty prominent technicians from 17 different developing countries visited Ringhalsverket in November 1986. Countries represented were Argentina, Ecuador, Jordan, Thailand, Uganda, Cuba and China. The technicians came to Sweden to study Swedish electricity supply. Swedpower was responsible for the arrangement and the program spanned two months and was arranged for the fourth year in a row. Swedpower shared experiences in the hydraulic engineering field with the participants. The course participants have made several study visits.

In 1986, Swedpower visited Saudi Arabia to help make the hot desert country's electricity grid more stable. Swedpower provided the training. Vattenfall hosted a UN seminar at the government's initiative to help the UN influence the energy and environmental situation in the world. 35 delegates and observers from around 40 countries. At Vattenfall in Råcksta there was a group that was collecting funds through salary deductions for, among other things, prisoners of conscience in Amnesty, AIDS and healthcare in Tanzania, etc.

Swedpower has installed power stations in Zimbabwe. Exported electricity accounts for the country's foreign exchange earnings. Farmers needed electricity for their water pumps to be able to harvest two or three crops. The state needed the foreign currency. Swedpower is helping the state-owned power company Electricite du Laos accelerate line construction. Swedpower was also in Mozambique and celebrated its 20th anniversary in 1999.

Since 1984, Sweden has provided 260 million SEK in energy assistance to Vietnam. An additional 200 million will be invested until 1998. A Vattenfall-er writes: "After many years of work, Swedpower has a good reputation and good contacts in Vietnam, and that is needed.

Competition for contracts is fierce now that the country is being electrified and the energy sector is being expanded." Swedpower in Zambia and Nicaragua. In Zambia, Swedpower worked with SIDA and Sweco.

Together with the World Childhood Foundation, Vattenfall has developed a program to help children in need for better living conditions such as housing, protection from sexual abuse, etc. Swedpower International has been working in Mozambique for over 20 years and the first contract was signed in 1979. The Swedish state and Vattenfall have developed a group that will be able to intervene and restore power lines in crisis areas. Vattenfall aided flooded areas in Elbe, Germany in 2002. The Tsunami victims also received disaster relief from Vattenfall, among others. In the Light at School project, Vattenfall in Poland works to provide schools with electricity and good lighting, so that students can have better conditions for studying.

Personnel policy

A corporation which cares about its customers and personnel is often also a successful competitor locally as well as globally. These issues are important within CSR because having a healthy workforce is key in being competitive and a sound employer.

Personnel policy - Shares

Ericsson

Share operations existed in both Ericsson and Trelleborg and were started during the 1970s and 1980s when interest in the savings form had increased. In 1983, 17% of the population, or nearly 1.3 million Swedes, owned shares. Sweden had thus overtaken the USA, where 15% of the population owned shares. In 1973, employees were invited to become shareholders in Ericsson. Approximately 900 employees in Sweden subscribed for 24.000 shares during the first two weeks. A shareholder association for the employees was established. In the 1980s, Ericsson established a cooperative savings fund for employees and their families. The company also offered loans at a five percent interest rate if employees also saved at least SEK 150 per month. There were also various training courses and information on how to invest in different forms of savings such as shares.

Trelleborg

During 1983, approximately three hundred Trelleborg employees had saved in Trelleborg shares. In 1984, Trelleborg employees subscribed to convertible bonds worth SEK 20 million, which were reserved for employees. The finance department at Trelleborg AB agreed with PK-bank, SE-Bank and Sparbanken that employees with a salary account could, after the usual credit check, borrow up to SEK 30.000 to be able to sign convertible bonds. There were over 19.000 shareholders in Trelleborg in 1988. Share savings among Trelleborg employees continued during the 1990s and bonuses were issued to all savers in 1992. Then a bonus system was introduced for everyone; white-collar workers, supervisors and collective employees to improve productivity in the company. The bonus was based on four components: productivity, sales, delivery precision and number of hours worked.

Personnel policy: Ceremonies in various forms

Ericsson

LM Day (after founder Lars Magnus Ericsson) was an event that started in the 1940s and became an annual celebration for employees and their families. The LM orchestra played, the theatre company showed off their skills, and LM sports teams also showed off during LM Day. During the 1940s, this day had around 6.000 visitors. Another activity that had its roots in the 1940s was the gold medal ceremony. This was an opportunity to celebrate employees who had worked for Ericsson, in some cases for more than 40 years. The festivities were characterized by "glamour" as 200 guests were invited, and it was held at the exclusive restaurant Gillet in Stockholm. The banquet was also framed with entertainment such as music and illusionists. Both blue-collar workers and white-collar workers were invited.

LM Day was also celebrated during the 1950s and was celebrated with families and friends of employees. In the 1950s, as many as 15,000 (1950) to 30,000 (1951) came to these events. These were accompanied by folk dancing, activities for children, the LM choir, the LME orchestra and sports.

During the 1960s, LM Day was a recurring celebration at Gröna Lund ("Grönan") in Stockholm. The party was surrounded by music, the LM orchestra, and folk dancing. Approximately 25.000 visitors came to Grönan. In addition, the LM Orchestra celebrated its 25th anniversary in 1963.

During the medal ceremony in 1972, 1.000 SEK went to the widows through Dr. Marcus Wallenberg's fund, and approximately 250.000 SEK in total had gone to the widows since 1968 when the fund was established. The medal ceremony continued into the 1970s when the men received gold watches and the women in turn received gold bracelets. The ceremony was also held at Stockholm City Hall, where the Nobel laureates also enjoyed their dinner.

The gold medal ceremony was held in 1981, for the 36th time, in Stockholm City Hall. The LM orchestra played, and the employees were offered an exclusive dinner. The LM Days were also held during the 1980s as well as the 1990s but were reduced to 7,000 visitors in 1995 and 1,800 in 1996. The reasons for this reduction were not found. The gold medal ceremony was framed by a luxurious dinner in Stockholm City Hall and live music during the 1990s

LM Day was preserved in the 21st century as an important tradition. Approximately 7,000 people participated in this event in 2005, although there was a large decline in the number of visitors compared to the 1950s. LM Day was introduced in Gothenburg in the 2000s, at Liseberg-park. The gold medal tradition was maintained in the 21st century.

Trelleborg

During the 1950s, Trelleborg also held a celebratory ceremony for its fiftieth anniversary where workers received increased pensions, funds were donated to the local educational institution, and 256 loyal servants were honoured. (December 10, 1956). In 1959, four loyal servants were celebrated who had a total of 160 years of service, the oldest being 77 years old. Trelleborg's veterans were honoured with flowers and gold watches after approximately 50 years of service with the company in 1966. A celebratory anniversary event was also held in Ulvsunda in 1969. One of the Engineering Club's annual traditional events was the Christmas tree looting party for the children of Trelleborg employees, and around 70 young people participated annually during the 1960s.

The ceremonies of the 1970s were not reported in the sources but must still have been a continuity in this work. There appear to have been summer trips for retirees who worked for the company during the 1970s. For the fourteenth time, "goodie bags" were distributed and Trelleborg invited its pensioners on a summer outing in 1981. Approximately 400 retirees participated. On October 29 of the same year, crystal bowls were awarded to loyal employees who had achieved 40 years of employment with the company, from Henry Dunker's holiday foundation and Trelleborg AB's personnel foundation.

In 1981, gold watches were also awarded to those who had completed 25 years of service with the company. The following year, 66 gold watches were awarded. Also in 1983, 40th anniversary toasts were given to about 20 employees. Gold watches were also awarded in 1983. In 1984, 19 loyal servants were awarded the 40-year trophy. Those who were able to celebrate 10 years with the company were also thanked and did so with a dinner and dance in the factory. A record number of gold watches were awarded in the group in 1985. Five Trelleborg residents received the gold watch in 1987 and celebrated at a cruise party. Also, in 1988 and 1989, people with 25 years of service in the company were thanked with gold watches.

In 1993, a 25th anniversary was celebrated in the Trelleborg Group for employees who had served the company for 25 and 40 years, respectively. Gold watches and crystal bowls were handed out. Two years later, a 90th anniversary was celebrated, including a share dividend. An exhibition at Trelleborg Museum also coincided with the anniversary. In 1996, the group companies Viking celebrated 100 years and Monarch 70 years, and it was celebrated at fancy hotels in tailcoats and dresses.

Vattenfall

Vattenfall organized a "family party" in Västerås in 1951 where employees were treated to entertainment and theatre. It was the initiative of the works councils and the safety committee. Kilforsen's Day was first organized in 1954 and was intended to return annually. The Västernorrland Regiment's music band performed, and the children received presents, and the whole day ended with dancing in Folkets hus. Kilforsen was inaugurated with celebration and joy in 1954, with Ådalsliden's lotto serving coffee and dip, Prince Bertil meeting with the county governor couple, and the whole thing ended with dinner and dancing. There was a royal splendour over Vattenfall's party at Stockholm City Hall when around 900 Vattenfall employees participated in the ceremony in 1959 to celebrate its fiftieth anniversary. The king, prime minister, cabinet ministers and others also participated. In the Golden Hall, approximately 40 meters of buffet tables awaited.

The Golden Helmet celebration continued throughout the 1960s. An accident commission and a central works council safety committee were established. These have provided courses to keep safety work up and injuries down. On November 22, 1968, it was time for a party in Råcksta again. The Golden Helmet went to four employees in 1969. Watch medal winners were recognized in the magazine in 1969 and for the first time, people could choose a gold watch instead of a service medal. In the same year, All Souls' Day was celebrated in Porjus by 300 people at the same time as a "Helyllefest" ("socially decent party") was celebrated in

Trollhättan. It was the inauguration of the then newly opened Oscars Bridge.

Golden Helmets were also awarded in 1970. Also medal celebrations for: "The reward (proof) for zeal and honesty in the service of the kingdom" was awarded in 1971. It was the king who handed out medals and watches to make it extra festive. Fallen's Day in Älvkarleby on June 19 and 20 (1971) was a major success. It was a "Folk Festival in the good old style" with ceremonial speeches, bands, folk dances, choirs, water skiing and local fiddlers framing the big attraction: the furious cascades of hydroelectric power down the Älvkarleby's cliffs.

Three young men of valour received the 1971 Golden Helmets. Truck driver Henry Norberg, 28 years old, Östen Johansson, 26 years old, and boat driver Per Harnesk, 22 years old, have all three shown great presence of mind and thereby saved lives. Four people received the Golden Helmet in 1972 for "long-standing interest in occupational safety and health." Gold watches were also awarded in a ceremonial manner at Råckstadgården on January 25, 1972. Medals were awarded to most employees in 1973 for zeal and integrity in the service of the kingdom. The Golden Helmet went to three deserving recipients and this time in 1973 it went to CFN's former chairman Karl-Hugo Carlsson. At Järvargården next to Piteå, Vattenfall had a farm for the staff at the Norrbotten power plant for employees who did leisure activities such as skiing.

In 1975, Fallen Days were organized in five places in Sweden – Porjus, Stornorrfors, Nämnforsen, Älvkarleby and Trollhättan. The crowd turnout was good. The Golden Helmet 1976; Safety Officer Kjell Mickelsson, Chief Engineer Gunnar Richson and Agency Director Birger Stridh. In 1976, Vattenfall had holiday resorts in Älvkarleby, among other places. 1976 Fallen Day – Folk Festival Day in Älvkarleby, Näsåker, Stornorrfors and Trollhättan.

The medal rain in 1976 was as usual abundant, no less than 189 Vattenfall workers received the medal for zeal and integrity in the service of the kingdom. Medals were also awarded the following year. Memorial Day was celebrated by 10.000 people in Näsåker in 1978 in a cultural and family-oriented day. These medal ceremonies and Memorial Day festivities continued throughout the decade.

Even during the 1980s, Vattenfall awarded gold medals or gold watches to most employees as an award for integrity in the service of the nation. In addition, four Vattenfall workers received the Golden Helmet, which is a courageous effort for occupational safety among the staff in 1980, 1981, 1984 and 1989, and probably also in the other years.

Personnel policy: Health-promoting strategies

Ericsson

A major responsibility for the company was to ensure that employees maintained good morale, to make them work more efficiently. There were many different sports that employees could get involved in: athletics, swimming, shooting, tennis, bowling, gymnastics, football, orienteering, bandy, skiing, handball, table tennis and wrestling.

During the 1960s, personnel policy changed, and articles highlighted "modern ergonomics". How office staff should design their "workstations" was described. The modern company's motive for care is to maintain good health among employees and, if necessary, restore health to those affected. It was in four areas that Ericsson had implemented their corporate healthcare: 1) Safety work to minimize damage to the machines. 2) Health checks to prevent injuries. 3-4) To group the workplace based on health risks and care for both staff and their families. Sports activities were maintained during the 1960s and there were major articles in Kontakten about boxing and cycling. Ericsson also started summer games for football and athletics.

Personnel policy and occupational health care were intensified during the period. A health council was established because of a negotiation between the social partners. The Health Board had a local role. From 1973, Ericsson offered "rest exercises" to reduce injuries from monotonous movements during working hours. Occupational health care had its embryonic start in the 1940s but had its major impact in the 1970s through debate in the media. During the 1970s, protective legislation for workers was implemented. The law meant that 20 percent of a company's profits would go to developing the work environment. This generated a fund of approximately 80 million kronor in 1975 monetary value. Ericsson also implemented training for staff to provide them with knowledge about chemical risks in the company.

The psychosocial situation of workers was on the agenda in 1981, when research had found that there was a positive correlation between the motivation and attitude of workers and the efficiency of the company. During the 1990s, a program was installed to improve electrical allergy symptoms. A committee was established to handle the situation and approximately two million Swedish kronor was invested to address the situation.

To make it easier for employees to access occupational health care, several telephone lines were opened in 2001 for them to call. In addition, Ericsson launched a campaign to encourage employees to exercise and reduce stress factors. The different activities were water aerobics, spinning, body pump and circuit gymnastics.

Trelleborg

Regarding noise and safety issues, Trelleborg, at the request of workers, had installed effective silencers on the bicycle department's compressor to reduce noise. Trelleborg had also issued protective masks to those working with zinc sulphate to reduce its harmful effects. Trelleborg had also applied to install mirrors and traffic signs in appropriate locations at intersections near the factory to reduce accidents. To increase occupational safety, management had also taken on the responsibility of communicating with all employees through letters to inform them of what needed to be done within the factory walls. In 1958, a modern machinery park, shower, sauna and air conditioning were installed in the Varberg branch to improve working conditions on site.

Because of the violent disease "The Asian" that ravaged the most in 1957 and 1958. Trelleborg saw to it that staff were given vaccines that came from England. The company physician, Yngve Rigerus, had procured vaccine for approximately 2.000 men.

In 1960, the group developed hearing protection to also dampen the sound from noisy industries and could withstand approximately 140 decibels. That is, quite high noise levels. The same hearing protection, "Supro," was later used by airline personnel in the United States. A power transmission protection system was developed in 1963 by Trelleborg to prevent serious accidents. To improve occupational safety, Trelleborg (Ljungby) has ensured that employees involved in the chemical production of plastics and rubber have access to protective masks and that several annual health checks are carried out. In Ljungby, gas tracking equipment had also been installed to keep accidents down. The company built a dining room and larger infirmary in the new staff building in 1965.

Through advice from negotiations between SAF and LO, Trelleborg had come to install a special council for occupational health care and employ an industrial physician. The council was made up of seven members, with industrial doctors, safety engineers and workers as elected representatives.

In 1976, Trelleborg had produced a new protective hood for small children at the initiative of the Swedish Civil Defence Agency, and approximately 300.000 were to be delivered between 1977 and 1979. The suit itself had a specially coated fabric that included both rubber and plastic. It has also been tested on children with the assistance of child psychologists. Nothing similar could be found in other countries at the time.

A number of work environment improvements had been made during 1970: for the Industrial Rubber Product Group, lighting conditions were improved, the production area was expanded by 250 square meters, resulting in more airy premises, all changing rooms were increased in capacity, including for women, the noise level was reduced by re-cladding the fan factories, and the smoking room and dining room were repainted.

For the Tires Product Group, the noise level of the fans was improved, the heating in the changing rooms and dining room was improved, washbasins were installed, and a new fan system was installed. For the Product Group "Preparation", vacuuming facilities were improved, ventilation was reviewed, noise insulation was installed, and the storage space was expanded.

When Trelleborg's new industrial hose factory was built in 1972, it was built with the latest in environmental protection and work environment, and the cost of this commitment was half the investment cost, that is, 2.5 out of 5 million SEK. Among other things, dust and noise measurements were installed, built-in lead management was installed, and the location of the factory was adapted to the requirements of the Swedish Environmental Protection Agency and the new Environmental Protection Act. Trelleborg informed about its work with vibration and noise reduction technologies at a Polish conference because it had worked on the issues previously and was well advanced in research in the area.

Trelleborg had invested in the fight against chemical health risks in 1982, where continuous work was carried out by safety representatives, safety engineers and company doctors. Examples of initiatives include the introduction of non-flammable solvents, the uptake of carcinogenic substances, etc. Trelleborg had initiated and carried out a large cancer survey in collaboration with LO and the Swedish Factory Workers' Union. This survey ran for six years and included just over 13.000 people. A new general health check was established in 1985–1986 for employees over 40 years of age. The examination included checking vision, hearing, blood pressure, blood sugar and blood lipids. Trelleborg initiated a Rehab project to rehabilitate the long-term ill and injured. This project was well-known and was visited by the Riksdag (Swedish Parliament) and the head of AMS. The idea was born during the county labour board's discussions with the company. Approximately SEK 50 million was allocated to special work environment initiatives within the group.

Approximately 50 million was invested in the work environment in 1990, with the money going to research and development regarding the environment and occupational safety, development of prototypes for machines and other equipment, and special projects in the most vulnerable workplaces. In 1992, an extra 11 million was invested in improving the working environment. Regarding the work environment, 6 million SEK in funding was distributed in 1990 to improve the work environment.

Vattenfall

The Swedish Water Authority's Support Fund (SVU) was established in 1932 on the initiative of some members of Vattenfall's board. The purpose of the association is to provide financial support to survivors of executives at Vattenfall who were financially dependent on the deceased, and to provide them with advice and assistance in financial matters. Every civil servant and worker who is or has been employed by the authority and pays an annual fee is a member of the association.

At a conference in 1952 in Stockholm with the building agency's safety inspectors, it was agreed to greatly intensify occupational safety and health to achieve a further decrease in the accident rate. In 1952, it was decided to implement a series of practical measures for more efficient protection work, including faster reporting and standardization of protective equipment.

In 1952, the benefit fund turned 20 when it was established to provide financial support for the survivors of Vattenfall employees. At a conference, accident risks and the role of safety representatives in this context were discussed, as organizations elsewhere were at the forefront of this work and Vattenfall's dangerous working conditions for builders prompted them to pay for the equipment that was considered necessary for safe work.

Since 1940, training for apprentices for operational services has been conducted at Vattenfall, and approximately 25 have been accepted per year, and the training was four years. Theoretical training was also included with mathematics and physics in secondary school skills and driver's license training was also included. The safety work in Stornorrfors was leading within Vattenfall where protective equipment (seatbelts, lifelines, eye protection, hearing protection, hard hats, rubber clothing, respiratory protection, etc.) was distributed at the workplace.

Vattenfall had installed a safety committee, local safety officers, chief safety officer and administrative safety department. Supervisors also received training in how to design occupational safety through boarding studies in Älvkarleby.

In 1967, Vattenfall received occupational health care for its employees, and a health care committee was established the same year. Occupational health care includes new employee examinations, health checks, assessments prior to job placement, selection for promotion, retraining and environmental monitoring.

A new ergonomics department established in 1970 dealt with issues of occupational hygiene, technical occupational safety, personal protective equipment, medical management of rehabilitation, and exercise and sports activities. The Committee for Occupational Health and Safety (UFA) held its first constituent meeting on October 21, 1970, and the silicosis hazard and the ergonomics issue were raised. A ceremony with the Golden Helmet was celebrated during the year. This was to draw attention to occupational safety in the group.

The Working Committee for Occupational Health and Safety took the initiative to train employees in occupational health and has tasked the ergonomics department and local safety officers with organizing extensive training in this area. A basic education program related to people, work and the work environment was installed in 1971. The Committee for Occupational Health and Safety (UFA) held a full-day conference in Råcksta on April 14, 1972 to discuss goals and means for occupational health care in Vattenfall. The meeting was also attended by the company's two occupational physicians, Bengt Zetterström and Stig Valentin. The 1972 medallists and the gold watch were awarded to staff during a festive ceremony for those celebrating. The Ergonomics and Safety Department held a course on personnel policy and occupational health care.

The revised Occupational Safety and Health Act, which came into effect on 1 January 1974, accelerated safety training within Vattenfall. The basic training of at least 20 hours in safety work that the law requires for safety personnel – especially safety representatives – has been organized in various ways in the workplace. The Golden Helmet of the Year 1975 went to line manager Alf Johansson, Technical Director Tage Olrog and first foreman Nils Sundqvist. In 1979, an ergonomic study of the work environment during inspections of hydroelectric power stations was started at Norrbotten Power Plant. The survey, which was the first of its kind within Vattenfall, was conducted in collaboration with Luleå University. Study circles were also initiated.

The employee benefit fund was established in 1932. The purpose is to provide financial support to employees, or their survivors, who have found themselves in a financially difficult situation due to health or other reasons. During 1980, a total of 2.,000 kronor was distributed. A board composed of parties decides whether to grant grants or loans.

Personnel policy: Gender equality, daycare and summer camp activities

Ericsson

When Ericsson expanded its production facilities by establishing Midsommarkransen, the need for daycare places for the workers' children increased. This initiative was because there were no daycare spaces at the new facility and the company had to respond to this need. The daycare was established in October 1940 and expanded during the first few years. Other activities for the children included the annual children's colony at Resarö in the Stockholm archipelago. This was free for the children because Ericsson covered the costs. A summer camp was also held at Steneby Castle in 1946. Approximately 60 to 80 children were allowed to spend the summers at the colony on Resarö. This was made permanent when Ericsson bought a house on the island for this business, Villa Ingbo. The purpose of the camp was for the children to be able to spend time in nature to recover from the hustle and bustle of the city. A handful of teachers met this need.

Even during the early 1960s, there was activity on Resarö, but in 1965 the death blow came when the business had to be closed due to too few children. However, the remainder of the operations were moved to Sörängen, also in the Stockholm archipelago.

Personnel policy during the 1990s increasingly focused on (gender and) equality issues. In 1995, Ericsson started a gender equality committee whose task was to change attitudes and shape opinion. They arranged conferences with around 140 participants from all over Sweden. Those who participated were decision-makers in the company, from the union, and human resources administrators. JämO, the Swedish state's gender equality ombudsman, initiated a campaign with the help of Ericsson to try to raise salaries for women. A new system for studying salary trends was developed to equalize these within the company. Free child insurance was established in the 1980s and could be used for all children of employees, and the basic insurance was 258,000 kronor in 1988.

The Croatian part of Ericsson was awarded a gender equality award for its work on gender equality issues. They had turned to the media to attract more women and get their messages out. This resulted in more women applying for positions at Ericsson. A quarter of all decision-makers and a third of all employees were women. This is after the action.

In Austria, Ericsson was a role model when it came to working on gender equality issues regarding women's childbirth. The women were given the opportunity to stay within the company and work a certain percentage and combine this with being at home with the children. It was considered important by Ericsson to continue to have access to women's expertise. Ericsson in Austria also established a meeting room with necessary changing tables and other facilities.

In Montreal, Canada, Ericsson installed a daycare centre in 1995 for the community. This was run by the employees and was sponsored by Ericsson and the local government.

Trelleborg

In 1970, "child parking" and childcare for employees within the group were established so that mothers and fathers would have time to perform tasks such as shopping or running other errands between 9:00 a.m. and 6:30 p.m. This service, premises and staff were provided by Trelleborg's Rubberfactory, and the capacity was around 20 to 30 children. A survey was conducted to map gender equality in the Trelleborg company back in 1984.

Gender equality was also discussed in the 1990s. In 1995, Trelleborg had set the framework for gender equality work in the company. The long-term goals are that women and men should be treated equally. Gender should not be a burden when it comes to employment, development and advancement. They wanted to take advantage of the unused resources available to employees. The issues were also discussed in the following years. In the same year, Trelleborg started training for managers to become better leaders and businesspeople under *STORM's Executive Programme.* Where 20 selected people would develop business games in business knowledge.

Vattenfall

In 1973, the situation of women was investigated within the state salary-regulated administration. It was considered that public employers had a major responsibility for the development towards equality between men and women in the workplace. The main task was to map conditions that counteract equality between men and women in the state-regulated labor market. Continuing to emphasize an article about parental leave published in Vi i Vattenfall in 1975 where the magazine discussed the possibility for men to be at home more with the children.

An equality day was organized in Råcksta on November 23, 1978. The issue of gender equality was no longer a private matter. The government has instructed the state agencies to set a good example and really do something about this issue. What is sought is, first and foremost, a change in attitude among both men and women. Activities such as study circle work were initiated. The debate emphasized raising women's low wages. Inger Nordlander was given responsibility for the gender equality function within Vattenfall from December 1979, and thus an official gender equality unit was established within the company. At Älvkarleby Power Plant in 1978, more fathers had been encouraged and taken the opportunity to share responsibility for caring for the children.

A typing course, for those interested, was organized to provide men and women with increased equality in the workplace. The equality group within Vattenfall was formed in the autumn of 1979 after three study circles on the subject of equality were held at the department in Råcksta. Vattenfall held its first weekly course on gender equality in the workplace and 12 women from Vattenfall gathered in Tällberg. The course content would provide increased self-confidence for the participants.

In the Motala power plant theme conference, a theme was held about women's salaries at Vattenfall and it turned out that the majority of women generally had a lower salary grade than men. Vattenfall thus gave 208 million to watercrafts municipalities to expand daycare places in these municipalities. Vattenfall has taken up and held training courses on gender equality and how prejudices, pay levels, etc. play a role in women's position in society. It has also been discussed that children should have a neutral upbringing so that women also choose technical professions.

Since Vattenfall is a state-owned company, corporate governance has allowed politics to have a hand in advancing gender equality in the company. For example, it was codified that gender equality would prevail in new hires. Vattenfall trains its managers, around 30, in gender equality work. Vattenfall attempted to strengthen gender equality by providing women with more internship opportunities in work areas typical of Vattenfall.

Vattenfall received a support and development group for its gender equality function. Both the executive board and all main departments are represented in the group. Provide information on current issues and support to line managers for increased gender equality - development of the institutions. Vattenfall established *the Gold Sign,* an award for work in gender equality, starting in 1985. Gold badge to employees in 1987 rewarded for gender equality. The 1988 Gold Sign was awarded to Hjördis Öhlund for efforts in the field of gender equality. That same year, a fair was held to increase interest in computers and technology among female employees.

Vattenfall helped create a leadership program, *RuterDam,* to bring more women into the business world. Just over 120 women from all over Europe gathered on Gotland through a European women's network, led by Marit Paulsen. The hosting was shared by Vattenfall and Assidomän.

Although welfare programs differ in the states in which Vattenfall operates, the Human Resources (HR) group at Vattenfall tries to ensure that personnel policies for employees are as uniform as possible, when it comes to parental leave and sick days. Vattenfall provides free healthcare and free medicines, and the company pays 80 percent of the main salary for those who are sick for more than 90 days.

In 2002, Vattenfall organized a seminar for 200 women who participated to improve their career opportunities. Women made up 24% of employees and only 13% of the management team. Vattenfall's deputy director believed that ethnic and gender diversity is important for Vattenfall to be able to compete for the best talent.

Personnel policy: Establishment of new communities

Vattenfall

When expanding the rivers, Vattenfall also founded communities to meet the needs of workers and white-collar workers. One such community was Harsprånget, where an absolute wilderness had been transformed into a city of 2,134 people with a construction time of one year (1952–1953). Associations were formed, study circles were initiated, and interest groups were started. Shops, a restaurant, an intercom and telegraph, a bus station, a playschool for children under school age, and a People's House were built. A school was also built in Harsprånget where around 90 children could be cared for. The older children who did not get a room were sent to the school in Porjus.

A community was also built in Stugun-Näverede. Bergeforsen was another community that was completed in 1955 for workers at Vattenfall, after the construction of the power station. However, Bergeforsen was already a community that was expanded with Vattenfall. Kilforsen is another example of the development that came to stand on the foundations of a pasture mound that was converted into a construction site in one year. Roads were built, followed by administrative buildings, the People's Hall, a hospital, schools and more. In Suorva, a different kind of school transport was organized where children were paid for a helicopter ride to school. In Porjus, the church was also renovated by Vattenfall, where, among other things, the altarpiece was a work by the artist Marianne Nordström from Stockholm. Near Storuman, Vattenfall built the community of Ajaure in 1960 in connection with the development of the rivers in Norrland. A school and a church were built.

Personnel policy: Corporate democracy and suggestion activities

Trelleborg

In collaboration with SAF, LO, TCO and Sveriges Radio, Trelleborg started a suggestion activity where employees can give a trip to the USA, Germany or the Nordic countries and also 5.000 SEK in pocket money. The suggestion activity would help to improve production. In 1959, a total of 231 employees at Trelleborgs Gummifabrik and its subsidiaries received 100 kronor as a vacation allowance, from Henry Dunkers' Vacation Foundation.

Trelleborg made sure to inform itself about suggestions for improvements in the factory from employees during the 1970s. The proposal activity in Trelleborg was active during the 1980s, where Denny Merkland received 10,000 kronor for providing a proposal that streamlined the production of so-called free-vulcanized hose. In 1984, more rewards were given for suggestions, with 198 people being rewarded with a total of just over 270.000 kronor. In 1985, Lars Andersson and Mikael Wingren were awarded 4.600 kronor for their proposals. Proposal activities developed strongly during the 1980s. In 1980, 283 proposals were submitted for assessment in Trelleborg and in 1989 the number of proposals had risen to 1266. In 1989, 691.000 SEK was awarded to the proposals. The proposal activity in Trelleborg continued during the 1990s and the total rewards were 700.000 SEK in 1992 when just over 1.100 proposals had been received. In 1994, 600.000 SEK was awarded to proposals that made operations more efficient to some extent.

Vattenfall

In 1948, a proposal award was established for measures to increase safety at work at Vattenfall. Approximately 5.000 SEK was allocated for this purpose in 1948 by Vattenfall. The new Occupational Safety and Health Act was discussed from the company's point of view. The suggestion activity at Vattenfall began in 1960, with staff being rewarded with 2.300 SEK for suggestions that could improve the organization and production. A course program for 700 safety representatives was introduced, for a sum of 200.000 SEK, the same year, where they were taught safety issues.

The proposal activity was also focused on occupational safety and approximately twelve proposals were rewarded with 2.625 SEK. Vattenfall gained a trusted physician in Bengt Hammarskjöld in 1959. In 1958 and 1959, golden helmets were awarded for faithful protection work. This was done under festive circumstances by Director General Erik Grafström.

In 1960, two golden helmets were awarded to those who worked on safety activities within Vattenfall, to recognize and reward active efforts for safety work. In 1962, Golden Helmets were awarded to Karl Johan Borgström and Karl Fredrik Ward for their part in the protection work.

The 1963 gold helmets went to three safety representatives because they had worked daily on work routines to increase the protection of personnel at Vattenfall. The 1964 Golden Helmets also went to three people.

A new form of corporate democracy was introduced in 1968 where personnel matters would become the preserve of all influence. Where more funds and corporate democracy would play a role in the business. Medical services and a research expert would be appointed as part of the decision. The new corporate democracy took effect when two positions on the board were expanded for employees within the agency. And a circulation between different professional categories would be incorporated.

The proposal activity continued in 1969, where three people shared 7.000 SEK to simplify work operations in the field. Health care was expanded, with ergonomics and occupational hygiene receiving two full-time specialist positions and occupational health care being included as an advisory expert function in the agency's personnel administration. Corporate Democracy included a group for personnel policy, local contact groups at works councils, more equal distribution of sports money, and staff representatives on the board. When planning for the newly built tire factory in 1970, the staff had been co-planners. Corporate democracy at Vattenfall was examined in 1970 at a joint plenum between workers and managers. That same year, five winners shared 5.000 kronor for their suggestions for streamlining operations.

In 1975, the new labour law legislation known as the Codetermination Act (MBL) was presented for the first time. A seminar was held at Råcksta about the state of corporate democracy. Starting in 1975, a system with personnel influence in employment matters was to be tested for two years. A fundamental point in the committee's proposal was that consultation on new employment issues should concern the entire decision-making chain that precedes the employment procedure.

Contacts between the agency and the employee organizations have become closer and deeper, but at the same time they have become more formalized, which means an increased workload.

Environmental work: From environmental price to energy saving

Environmental work is among the crucial factors within CSR to become a business player that is understanding the planetary situation in the current state. Caring to our joint green issues are equally important as every issue within CSR and sustainability.

Ericsson

Environmental issues began to engage Ericsson in the 1970s. In 1972, Ericsson won an environmental award established by the Swedish business community. The company received the award because it had cleaned the emissions from its factories into waterways. Ericsson also influenced Helios in 1974, another company, to reduce its environmental emissions from its factories.

Environmental issues were also relevant during the 1980s and in a campaign, Ericsson wanted to bring about a change in the Stockholm archipelago so that it was kept clean. Employees were motivated to take responsibility when using nature. This campaign was spread with posters and advertisements and was initiated 10 years earlier.

During the 1990s, Ericsson began discussing circularity and recycling of materials. Because of this, Ericsson created a new unit for the environment. This environmental group had four main goals for its activities: 1) to respond to policy issues and conduct environmental analyses 2) to conduct environmental audits of the factories and collect data on environmental damage 3) to respond to internal and external communication issues in the environmental area 4) to create an environmental report. This resulted in Ericsson being among the first to stop using freons in its manufacturing processes.

By working with the environmental reports, Ericsson adopted the International Chamber of Commerce's Business Charter for Sustainable Development. When Ericsson built an office in Nacka, Stockholm, they used their environmental policy to initiate operations to sort glass, paper and other materials. Later, Ericsson developed a new method they called environmental life cycle analysis, where they tested the impact of products on the external environment.

When a stakeholder – the Östergötland County Administrative Board – wanted Ericsson to reduce its emissions and environmental toxins from the Ingelsta factory in Norrköping, Ericsson developed a new system for this. Ericsson developed an innovative solution where solvents were filtered through organic material and worms. The effect was a reduction from 33 to three tons of solvent. The process spread to other factories in Sweden. For the invention of this process, Ericsson received the prestigious award: British Telecom's Environmental Prize.

Ericsson participated in the environmental train that travelled around the country and highlighted new methods for having a modern and environmentally friendly office. Ericsson collaborated with the Swedish Society for Nature Conservation, Nutek and TCO with efficient lighting resources and pens made from recycled materials.

To highlight environmental issues, Ericsson invested in environmentally friendly packaging for mobile phones. This research was conducted in Lund. The result of the research was a reduced amount of paper and plastic used in packaging, which also made transportation more efficient.

The first environmental policy was written in the 1990s and was an introduction to today's producer responsibility. The life cycle perspective was the crucial component of this work (see above). The life cycle perspective was developed at Chalmers and the Institute for Water and Air Quality Research. The ISO collaboration has given the Swedish companies and Ericsson the task of leading the work on the standardization of the life cycle process. To evaluate the work with the environment, data is collected and analyzed. In this work with environmental certifications, Ericsson was among the first Swedish companies to implement ISO-9000 and ISO-14001. The first environmental certificate went to the factory in Scunthorpe, England in 1996.

Ericsson in India was also among the first to implement ISO-9000 and ISO-14001. This is a long-term strategy for Ericsson, which wants to become a pioneer in environmental work. In India, Ericsson was also the first to do this work. Ericsson also recruited personnel in Japan and Southeast Asia who would have expertise in the environmental field. To spread the message of ISO-14001, Ericsson organized an interactive theatre and lectures on the subject. In 1997, Ericsson arranged a meeting for all environmental managers throughout the group to discuss the future in the environmental area. This conference was held in Madrid. The first facility to be environmentally certified in Sweden was the factory in Hudiksvall, and Ericsson was fully certified around 2000.

Ericsson is one of the first large companies with all units within the group certified to ISO-14001. All dimensions of ISO-14001 and all operations are also certified and evaluated.

Ericsson started by taking over the recycling of used products returned to retailers. Ericsson did the recycling themselves and expected to make a profit on the coup. The company was also involved in delivering the control computer for a satellite that would monitor the environment from space. Ericsson invented a computer module that did not require lead to manufacture, which changed the environmental work at Ericsson.

Trelleborg

In 1970, a program was launched to measure emissions of smoke, noise and gas from factories. The measurement program was drawn up in collaboration with the Swedish Environmental Protection Agency and was intended to reduce emissions from the factories. With the same caring purpose, Trelleborg's Rubberfactory has used a more expensive special fuel for forklifts and other diesel-powered vehicles because it emits less sulphur dioxide and creates cleaner air. When a new factory was established in Landskrona in 1972, it had undergone a thorough review regarding high demands on the environment and occupational safety.

Upon demand, Trelleborgsplast made a whole series of environmental products for waste oil, waste, garbage, industrial cooling water and rest areas in 1972. According to the article in Trelleborgsnyheter in 1972, Trelleborg has combated noise, dust and corrosion in the work environment and, in the external environment, invented an oil bilge to combat oil leaks. Trelleborg has been involved in developing Sweden's first environmental protection vehicle for combating disaster hotspots. This was at the initiative of several Skåne municipalities, who invested half a million in the project in 1976. Trelleborg manufactured 10 chemical protective suits that belonged to the car.

In 1977, Trelleborg developed an environmentally friendly chemical hose that handled 95% of all chemicals without problems. Trell-Chem, as the hose was called, had a middle layer of specially composed rubber and extra reinforcement with polyester yarn.

In 1981, energy savings were made with better sealing. Trelleborg's waste management was recognized by the Trelleborg Health Agency as one of the best in the country, including handling oil residues, rubber solutions and other mixtures. In 1984, the waste management system, which had already been praised, was updated. Ventilation was improved in 1987, making it more energy efficient. Lead emissions had been "significantly" reduced and were well below the current permit level, and several million kronor were planned to reduce the levels further.

On the environmental front, a significant amount was invested and discovered during the 1990s, and most articles in the staff magazines were about the external environment. For example, management had a development day in Smygehuk in 1990 to discuss the environment within the group. In the Ystad factory, new ventilation was installed for handling solvents, which cost around 4 million kronor in 1990. Approximately 2.25 million went to the manufacture of tires to make production more environmentally friendly.

At the turn of the year 1992, the hose factory in Trelleborg switched to source sorting of its waste. Containers were set up around the factory and clear signs were put up to show what should be thrown away where. The factory's location in the city of Trelleborg meant that strict requirements were created regarding the external environment and emissions, and Trelleborg investigated issues regarding emissions, including solvents and dust, in 1992. In 1993, new filters in the Trelleborg facilities reduced their emissions from just over 70 tons to 10 tons of solvent. An accident triggered this venture. Waste sorting was made more efficient in 1994, and around 60 percent of the materials deposited were recycled. New procedures regarding internal environmental audits were established in 1995. In 1995, the Trelleborg Group signed up to the idea and action program "Responsibility and Care", which means methodically testing its ideas against its own operations and trying to apply them in active action when it comes to environmental issues.

Trelleborg Monarch was named Company of the Year for their work with ISO certification in 1995. Trelleborg Viking in Norway succeeded in saving electricity, heating and water. By controlling how heat, water and electricity are used, they have already been able to save over one million (Norwegian) kronor in the first year.

In 1995, there was discussion about whether ISO or EMS should form the basis for environmental certification within the company (ISO 14000). In 1995, an environmental policy (CSR) was also established with a goal-oriented environmental work as a basis. Trelleborg had environmentally friendly products in its range early on (1995), where in Höganäs and Värnamo they were able to offer seals for windows and rubber sheets that prevent landfills from polluting local water. The proposal activity was also focused on achieving more environmentally friendly production, and 41.000 SEK was awarded to an individual at the company in 1996.

A network for environmental work was formed at Trelleborg for companies in Sweden and Norway. Trelleborg Viking was Trelleborg's first environmentally certified company (1997) within the group, with ISO 14001 certification. This consists of five different parts: environmental management system, environmental audit, environmental performance, life cycle assessment and ecolabelling. Trelleborg Viking was at the forefront of environmental certification in the Nordic region, and customers, such as Volvo, began to suggest that requirements would be tightened and that the authorities in Norway had looked at the water quality in the area, which inspired the company to take environmental initiatives. Above all, it was the threat of laws and regulations that eluded them that made the company take charge of its own environmental management. The profit argument was also used to justify investing in the environment. In 1997, there were plans for the entire operation to be ISO certified within two years, which was also achieved.

Trelleborg had further developed its environmentally friendly products with the Twin Tyre tire that reduces soil damage in agriculture and forestry, rubber strips for windows and doors that provide energy savings, and the Durolam sandwich material that reduces noise and vibrations. In 2002, environmental investments amounted to approximately 9 percent or approximately SEK 61 million. Trelleborg received high marks for its 2002 environmental report from the business community.

In Clermont-Ferrand, one of Trelleborg's largest facilities in France, received a new energy facility that made major cost savings in 2003. Among Trelleborg's facilities, 82 units in 19 countries were environmentally certified according to the ISO standard in 2003. Environmental work in Malta was rewarded with an award by the local authorities in 2004. Trelleborg was also awarded in 2005 for its environmental work, including for organizing environmental and risk management within the organization. The Group's environmental function will serve as a knowledge center on environmental issues and act as support for the business areas. In 2008, water was discussed as an important part of Trelleborg's environmental work and they are working to manufacture efficient and leak-proof hoses that can transport waste and more without endangering the environment. Also in 2009, new product types were discussed in the hose area, making them even more durable than before.

Vattenfall

When it comes to environmental issues, Vattenfall was early in ensuring that fish farms were planted to maintain fishing when expanding hydropower. The expansion was supervised by all sorts of experts, professors in fisheries issues, the Swedish Forestry University and SMHI. During the expansion of the Torne River and other rivers, fishing was compensated with 100 million in measures to maintain a certain quota of fishing. When it comes to nuclear power, Vattenfall advocated for its expansion, especially during the 1960s. In 1969, Vattenfall established an environmental foundation for technical and scientific research to protect and improve the external environmental conditions in society in terms of water, air and natural conditions. The foundation had over 2 million kronor at its disposal. Vattenfall released approximately 600,000 salmon fry per year in 1968. Vattenfall advocated for cities to switch to electricity and district heating instead of oil in order to become more environmentally friendly.

Vattenfall established an environmental foundation in 1969, which held its second meeting on February 9, 1970. Their credo was that water, air and nature should be protected and improved. The purpose of the foundation is to promote technical scientific research with the aim of contributing, in connection with activities mainly in the field of electrical energy, to protecting and improving the external environmental conditions in society through water, air and nature conservation.

Because environmental protection was linked to the power industry's operations, Vattenfall and others formed an environmental protection committee that became operational on January 13, 1931. Its main task was to promote environmentally friendly solutions for power expansion within the framework of the power industry's objectives. By mapping and studying the impact of power expansions on the environment, a basis is obtained for a common environmental policy for the power industry. Fish farming continued during the period and a Salmon Research Institute and the State Fish Farming Institute had been established in the area.

In 1975, 50,000 trout and 53,000 salmon were released into the river and one of the institution's – the Swedish state's fish farming institution - most important tasks is to keep endangered trout stocks alive in certain watercourses in Sweden. Vattenfall invested 60 million in the Stenungssund's power plant to improve the internal and external environment. Vattenfall participated in a unique environmental control program together with the municipality and the petrochemical industry.

In 1982, Vattenfall developed electric cars to develop the technology. The state had provided funds for this initiative. Vattenfall also had many flatbed mopeds powered by electricity in their stable because they wanted to save on gasoline. Vattenfall had an environmental policy from 1987, a balance between what is technically possible, what is ecologically justified and what is economically reasonable. The proposal was prepared by the company and the union and reviewed by the Swedish Environmental Protection Agency. The document presents a fundamental approach that, among other things, means striving for interaction between natural resources, the environment, technology and economics and benefit in Vattenfall's operations.

In 1988, Vattenfall focused on communicating environmental issues, so that they would be spread throughout the company. Next on the agenda was extensive environmental training for all personnel who encounter environmental issues daily. The training should both change attitudes and teach what rules and restrictions apply to ensure that nature is not burdened more than it can bear. At the Vattenfall symposium held in Stockholm in 1989, there was a vision that the environment would become a future business area. Vattenfall arranged a seminar on the greenhouse effect in 1989.

Vattenfall was involved at Lake Hornborga together with the Swedish Environmental Protection Agency to restore the habitat for birds. The lake had almost been wiped out. Several bird species could be saved. Vattenfall believes that nuclear power is good for the environment. HEW Environmental Foundation was established in 1994 as an environmental organization to support projects in nature conservation and environmental education for Vattenfall employees.

Vattenfall established the environmentally focused certification tool ISO 14001 in its operations, which was established in 2000 but started in the 1990s. From having concentrated environmental efforts on emissions issues and local environmental issues around its own facilities,

Vattenfall took the full step and integrated environmental aspects into the Group's operations. The 1995 environmental report was the first published by the group.

New and more modern cables were developed by Vattenfall and ABB, among others, and they are completely recyclable and 10 to 15 percent cheaper than older types of cables. Vattenfall has invested billions over the next 10 years (2000) to improve their environmental work. Vattenfall was the first company in the world to test a new system for offshore wind power. Specialists from the Swedish and German organization group in Vattenfall to research a carbon-free power station. Upgrading the Finnish Pamilo hydroelectric plant was part of Vattenfall's strategy to create reusable energy production. An alliance between Chalmers and Vattenfall and other international universities and companies was created to create a sustainable future. These are to develop new technologies for a sustainable future. Vattenfall is participating in an international campaign to combat global warming. Vattenfall presented its CSR ideas to the United Nations (UN) Commission on Sustainable Development. Customers and the environment are two important stakeholders that Vattenfall works towards.

Vattenfall has developed a system for converting waste into energy. Vattenfall influences its customers, such as Holmen Paper, to reduce their consumption of electricity – *Process* Efficiency Cooperation. Vattenfall is helping in Malaysia to reduce industry's carbon dioxide waste. Vattenfall has received an award for carbon dioxide separation in Germany. In the same project, Vattenfall had the ambition to reduce carbon dioxide emissions in coal production to zero by 2050. Vattenfall was in Ukraine as a consultant to get their point that reducing costs is equated with saving energy.

Understanding the concept of CSR

As a concept CSR has landed within the corporate and business sphere. There is a difference between Implicit and Explicit CSR even though this difference is downplayed due to globalisation. All the studied businesses have catered to the concept but in a later stage more explicitly than their implicit past.

Ericsson, Trelleborg & Vattenfall

During the 1970s, Vattenfall began discussing the importance of reporting on social factors, to demonstrate the company's importance in these issues. This article in the company newspaper came from the debate that erupted after Pehr Gyllenhammar, then Volvo's CEO, published an opinion article in Dagens Nyheter. This article had debated these issues.

During the 1980s, Trelleborg, along with several entrepreneurs, established an ethics committee that would test the health aspects of chemical products for the chemical industry. This indicates an increased understanding by the company of societal demands. At Vattenfall, the discussion of social issues continued with a Q&A with ethics professor Peter Kostenbaum from the University of San Jose.

During the 1990s, understanding of CSR increased when Ericsson used synonyms for the concept such as "Corporate Citizenship" to demonstrate the social responsibility of companies. The concept meant that companies were seen as having citizenship. The article showed the lack of a conscious practice, even though one has existed in the company. Vattenfall established its first responsible role in the company for environmental and social issues around 1990–1999, which shows that the company started its work with a conscious strategy.

During the 2000s, companies developed a greater understanding of CSR when, for example, Ericsson established a code of conduct for the first time, a framework for ethical behaviour when it came to human rights, collective bargaining and discrimination in 2001. The following year, the first official CSR report came from Ericsson. In addition, an interactive website for questions was added in 2006 for the company and its stakeholders. During the same period, Trelleborg also established a code of conduct (2002).

Vattenfall developed a code of conduct the same year as Ericsson and established its first CSR report (2004). Vattenfall's ambitions in this code of conduct pointed to its industry affiliation and product as the main understanding for CSR work. This foundation rests on their environmental impact when creating energy and power from nature and that they evaluate these insights in new investments. CSR is seen to be transparent about social and environmental issues.

Analytical discussion

Summary & comments

Corporate Social Responsibility (CSR) exploded in the early 2000s with the number of sustainability reports and statements from companies. In the new capitalist order, companies would work with responsibility and the creation of trust in society by communicating externally and internally what companies were doing about environmental, social and economic problems in society. Problems that had been created by the industry or by the company itself, in its actions.

In this book I have studied three large Swedish companies and their CSR history and practice from around 1940 to 2010. The book is based on ideas about a free but responsible business community that is a natural part of a pluralistic society. It is thanks to pluralism, the market and democracy that we have a strong society in Sweden. Not just state. Not just the market. Not just companies. This reflects a view of society where institutions and norms under capitalism are not only regulated by laws but also by the self-awareness of doing good. With influence comes responsibility.

Sponsorship of culture, sports and education

Culture, sports and sponsorship have frequent conflicts with, among other things, health work in personnel policy, since sports activities could improve the health of the staff. There are also similarities with the company security and company fire brigade because their work in service sometimes involved tommy-gun shooting and ski training in the north!

The culture that was sponsored was museum activities throughout all three companies. Ericsson helped create Lars Magnus Ericsson's Museum in Värmskog after the company's founder, where they also collaborated with local heritage organizations. Trelleborg joined other companies in the salvage of Vasa, when the Swedish state was initially uninterested. The result of this was the popular Vasa Museum in the royal capital. Trelleborg also installed an art association at the headquarters. Vattenfall sponsored the Theatre "Dramaten" in various contexts.

When it came to sports, there was everything within the organization such as aerobics, badminton shooting and tennis to name a few activities that the staff could get involved in. For those who liked gymnastics, they could "Spänsta med Roland", ("Flex with Roland") Vattenfall's jovial Vice President in the 1960s. Sports sponsorship was also included in Trelleborg, where tires and motorsports in various forms were sponsored; motocross, Formula 1 and rally.

Companies were also diligent in providing funds for scholarships and research grants to youth and young adults.

Corporate security and corporate fire brigade

In this matter, companies assisted the state during World War II and during the Cold War by being part of the defense of Sweden. Not exactly what is discussed as CSR and CSR in general. However, this is a way to supplement the total defense and home defense and be able to defend the factories and headquarters themselves if war should occur. This corporate security/operational security was part of the Home Guard and cooperation with the total defense was carried out during working hours.

The Swedish Corporate Defense Fund collected money for our Nordic neighbours during the 1940s to assist in wartime. There was a gender division where men were active in the military while women assisted with food and supplies in the Lotta corps. The company security forces practiced shooting and training in inaccessible nature. Otherwise, Ericsson was part of the high guard and Trelleborg had developed a shoot-and-throw weapon through close cooperation with the government. The company security existed until the 1980s.

There was also a company fire brigade in the companies that had close ties with the company security service, and these were established during the 1940s and 1950s and later merged into the municipal fire brigade (around 1970-1980). Before that, the company fire department was responsible for its own facilities but could also assist the municipal fire department in the event of major disasters in peacetime and wartime. There was thus a supporting role at the municipal level and cooperation with the national Armed Forces. This becomes CSR because it is about what the state, civil society and companies do for the good of the nation.

Aid and poverty alleviation

There are three major analytical trends in corporate and personnel magazines when it comes to aid and poverty alleviation: 1) the core business principle 2) that there are early established relationships with non-governmental organizations such as the Red Cross, 3) over time there is an establishment of previous practice in institutionalizing the activities.

Using the core business principle is important according to modern theories around CSR. Certainly, resources were donated to countries during World War II (1940s) such as Norway and the Netherlands, and Hungary received financial funds during the 1950s. It was only with the support to Cali in Colombia when replacing the community's telecommunications system after an earthquake in 1956 that Ericsson used the core business principle for the first time. Vattenfall acted on this principle – core business – and supported Pakistan and Ethiopia with its expertise in electricity and power supply in East Pakistan. A third example of this is the collaboration between the Swedish development agency SIDA and Vattenfall when eleven engineers organized and performed service on a dam facility in Kaufe Gorge Zambia. One of the biggest responsibilities in the development assistance issue was to transfer knowledge on how a hydroelectric power plant would be controlled and managed. The collaboration between Vattenfall and SIDA continued in 1974, when two engineers travelled to Kenya to support local knowledge of operating hydroelectric power plants. Sri Lanka also received this support in 1979. The core business principle was established over the decades and a modern example of this was when Ericsson distributed GSM systems to disaster-stricken areas in China and Albania. Where telephone networks were replaced after storms and was a collaboration between Ericsson and the Red Cross.

To illustrate the difference with an example of international aid that did not support core operations, Trelleborg's collaboration with Radiohjälpen – a Swedish aid organization. After an earthquake in Agadir, victims of the devastation were helped with clothes, food, cutlery and so on. This was not in line with the core value principle because it was not within the company's specialization or expertise.

The institutionalization of aid and poverty alleviation can be seen in the development from loose and sporadic organization to external communication and action as in the cases of Swedpower (Vattenfall) and Ericsson Response (Ericsson). *Women in Vattenfall* (KIV) helped Hungarian refugees in 1956 with housing, clothing and toys for these refugees, and the company donated 54.000 kronor to support the Hungarian Fundraising. However, this formation disappeared to some extent and perhaps returned in personnel policy in view of Vattenfall's gender equality work and with the establishment of Swedpower (1980) for the development assistance organization. A first mission for the organization was to contribute to local hydropower in Mozambique. Swedpower also arranged training courses in Sweden for international guests and delegates from 17 different developing countries, in Stockholm. For twenty years, development in Mozambique was supported, although there was a measure of altruism, as it was described in the staff magazine that these investments in the country could contribute to future contracts and profits for the company.

The LMs' Developing Countries Association (LMU) was established in 1976 in Ericsson with the ambition and goal of contributing to a richer world between developing and industrialized countries. LMU concentrated its activities on projects in developing countries. They collaborated with various non-governmental organizations such as Save the Children and Amnesty International. There were four projects that were prioritized initially: 1) the implementation of a flour mill for Brazilian farmers, 2) the installation of a hospital for leprosy-stricken children in Yemen, 3) food and medicine for southern Yemen, and 4) donations to schools in Rhodesia. LMU also acted when tsunamis hit Thailand in 1979, affecting 100.000 people. Approximately 100 local Ericsson employees were involved in collecting medicine, money, food, salt and clothing. LMU stagnated during the 1980s due to declining membership. The tradition of aid continued, albeit later. In 2001, *Ericsson initiated the intra-organization Ericsson Response*, a modern aid agency.

A document was signed between the United Nations (UN) and Ericsson in which Ericsson guaranteed to contribute GSM technology to the UN Communications Headquarters in Brindisi, the United Nations Office for the Coordination of Humanitarian Affairs. This communication technology greased the communication wheels for the UN. An important historic contract was signed in 2002 between Ericsson Response and the Red Cross. This unique document involved sharing knowledge and personnel in disasters to reduce risks. Ericsson Response applied the core value principle in disasters such as September 11, 2001 (New York),

Hurricane Catharina and an earthquake in Pakistan with 30.000 victims, and the Tsunami in Southeast Asia in 2005.

Already at the beginning of the period under investigation, the troika of large Swedish companies had become involved in aid and poverty alleviation, in countries such as the Netherlands and Colombia. KIV in Vattenfall was established in 1929 and increased its powers with the Hungarian refugees during the 1950s. This initiative transformed into Swedpower, which came to work with the core value principle and aid during the 1970s. NGOs that collaborated with large Swedish companies early on were the Red Cross and Save the Children. LMU was active between 1976 and 1981 with aid and was replaced by Ericsson Response, which worked with Tsunami victims in 2005, among other things. There are altruistic but also purely profit motives when it comes to these activities. This is not very controversial as companies must make a profit to develop and survive in the long term.

Personnel policy

The personnel policy included share activities, ceremonies, health promotion strategies, equality, daycare and colony activities, establishment of new communities, as well as corporate democracy and suggestion activities.

The share operation seems to have been a way to popularize ownership by giving employees themselves incentives to participate and create value in the companies. These initiatives were most widely publicized during the late 1970s and 1980s. This can perhaps be seen as a normative transfer of knowledge in savings, much like with microfinance.

Some of the ceremonies that existed were LM Day, Fallen Day, Golden Bell and medal ceremonies in the troika of surveyed companies. These were a way to create context internally so that employees would feel involved and the companies would feel like a family, and a way to create local support. But also, for companies to be exposed externally, a form of external communication. CSR is, at its core, communication in companies, considering the sustainability reports that are published today but also for the company magazines that were created for internal communication (on which this study is based).

When it comes to health-promoting strategies, the companies surveyed had different strategies. Ericsson started with a smorgasbord of activities such as athletics, swimming, shooting, tennis and so on to keep the staff in good spirits. Ergonomics and how the office should be functional was another strategy. A health council consisting of the social partners was institutionalized and developed during the 1970s to disseminate knowledge and work on new legislation in the area. Understanding of the psychosocial environment was also improved by a helpline launched in the early 2000s, although the issue had been discussed earlier. In Trelleborg, occupational health care was also institutionalized with a council consisting of the social partners and an industrial physician. However, occupational health care had evolved with noise issues and the international pandemic Asian. Later, fan systems, ventilation and improved noise levels in the factories were also phased into the company's production units in the chemical industry to which the company belonged. Improving noise levels runs like a common thread through the company's work with health-promoting strategies. A restriction on the use of various chemicals and increased insight into carcinogenic substances also came during the 1980s. Since the 1930s, Vattenfall had established a system through the Swedish Waterworks Authority's Support Fund to compensate families who had suffered an accident at work. As early as the 1940s, safety work at Vattenfall was extensive, with various forms of protective equipment available at workplaces in the company. It involved eye protection, hearing protection, safety helmets, rubber clothing and respiratory protection. In 1967, safety work at Vattenfall was institutionalized and an occupational health service was established. In 1970, a new ergonomics department was established and in the same year a committee for occupational health and safety was established. Legislation from 1974 also intensified occupational safety and health.

All three companies worked on gender equality issues. Ericsson, which found its way into an international arena and inspired gender equality issues in countries such as Austria, Croatia and Canada. Ericsson started a gender equality committee in 1995, which organized conferences and meetings to form opinions and understanding of the issues. Trelleborg was late to embrace the issues, but in 1995 it started a leadership training program for women. If Trelleborg was the least committed to the issues, Vattenfall was the company that worked the most on gender equality. Women in Vattenfall was one of the earliest organizations established in the 1930s, which is likely why they apparently influenced the company on these issues. Vattenfall's previous state control also had an impact on the company, which is now incorporated. As early as the 1970s, gender equality conditions in the company were mapped. There was also discussion about how fathers would be given the opportunity to be at home with their children. Salary levels were mapped, employees were trained in equality work, the RuterDam network was established and a person responsible (Inger Nordlander) for the issues was appointed in the company, in comparison to how there is a CSR or sustainability manager today.

When it comes to establishing new communities, it was Vattenfall that had the demand to expand the Swedish community by establishing these near power plant construction sites. They established schools, shops, restaurant, bus station for these communities to function. Bergeforsen, Harsprånget, Stugun-Näverede and Ajaure were examples of such communities.

With the corporate democracy reforms of the 1970s, such as the Codetermination Act (MBL), companies also began to implement this in their operations. Ericsson did not express this internally, while the state-owned Vattenfall had already informed employees about personnel issues in 1968. Instead, Trelleborg had a comprehensive proposal process that was rewarded. During the 1970s, Vattenfall continued to develop corporate democracy with joint plenums and co-planners. It can therefore be seen that industry-specific and ownership conditions affect CSR content, as Vattenfall stands out in gender equality and corporate democracy reform work.

Environmental work

Ericsson has worked on environmental issues since the 1970s and won many awards, for example in 1972 from the Swedish business community and the prestigious British Telecom's Environmental Prize during the 1990s. Ericsson institutionalized environmental work and also responded to stakeholders' interests in the local environment, such as in the case of the Östergötland County Administrative Board over the factory in Norrköping, which demonstrates the company's responsibility in the matter. Ericsson was also the first in an international arena to implement environmental work according to ISO-9000 and ISO-14001 in India.

Trelleborg also had environmental awareness from the 1970s when establishing new factories, ensuring that emissions of smoke, gas and noise were improved by measuring them. Since the company operates in the chemical industry, great care was taken to ensure that the purification of the chemical processes would keep emissions of lead and oil at low levels. The year 1995 appears to be a clear intensification of environmental work when, among other things, environmental auditors were established and environmental certification according to ISO-14001 was established. The company continued to work with the materials in the manufacturing process and during the 2000s, the more environmentally friendly Twin Tyre was introduced, which reduced soil damage in agriculture and forestry. Looking at the whole, environmental work was mainly directed at chemical processes, chemicals and various materials.

Vattenfall worked on different types of environmental issues. One of the key issues was to ensure that there were vibrant fish farms in connection with the expansion of hydroelectric power. There they collaborated with the Swedish School of Forestry and the Swedish Meteorological and Hydrological Institute (SMHI). For the expansion of the Torne River, fishing was compensated with 100 million SEK. In collaboration with the Salmon Research Institute and the State Fish Farming Institute, the company attempted to release 50,000 trout and 53,000 salmon from fish farms into the river. During the early 1980s, work was also underway to develop an electric car to develop the technology. They established ISO-14001 in their operations in 2000. Then I joined German partners in a project to research carbon-free power stations. What perhaps determined this work was Vattenfall's early institutionalization of environmental issues in 1969, where an environmental foundation for technical research was established. However, there was an ambivalence regarding the non-existence or existence of nuclear power.

The CSR concept

Already in the 1970s, Vattenfall began discussing the importance of social reporting with Pehr Gyllenhammar's article. The companies surveyed were thus already aware of CSR in the 1970s. Even in the Trelleborg sphere, an ethics committee was established in the 1980s to discuss aspects of the chemical industry. In the 1990s, understanding of CSR increased even more when Ericsson used synonyms for the concept such as "Corporate Citizenship", which simply means that companies are seen as having citizenship. However, it would have to wait until the end of the decade when these companies had a conscious strategy, even if they worked with broad social responsibility during the period under study. The externally communicated sustainability reports and code of conduct came in the 2000s; Ericsson in 2001, Trelleborg in 2002 and Vattenfall in 2004. This increased transparency in CSR issues internally but also externally.

Sources and further reading

Staff magazines:
Ericsson: "Kontakten", 1940 – 2006

Trelleborg: "Trelleborg-Nytt, T-snabben, T-blandning och T-time", 1953–2010

Vattenfall: "Energitidningen och Euroenergy", 1940 – 2010.

"Kvinnor i Vattenfall" – KIV. By Ingela Näslund, archivist Vattenfall, april 2010

Further Reading:
Aspegren Carl (2005), *De första 100-åren*. Trelleborg AB.

Carroll Archie B, Lipartito Kenneth, Post James E. & Werhane Patricia H. (2012), *Corporate Responsibility*. Cambridge.

De Geer Hans (2008), "Den svenska historien, modellen och förståelsen för CSR". Nilsson, Torun (2008), *125 år med Corporate Social Responsibility*. Centrum för Näringslivshistoria.

Rhenman, Eric (1964), *Företagsdemokrati och företagsorganisation*. Norstedts.

Ihlen Oyvind & von Weltzien Hoivik (2013), Ye Olde CSR: The historic roots of Corporate Social Responsibility in Norway. I *Journal of Business Ethics*, 127: 109-120.

Lalander Sven (1984), *Vattenfall under 75 år: 1909-1984*. Statens vattenfallsverk.

Lee, Min-Dong Paul (2008), A review of the theories of Corporate Social Responsibility: Its evolutionary path and the road ahead. *International journal of Management Reviews*, 10(1): 53-73

Lundström, Brita (2006) Grundat 1876: *Historia och företagsidentitet inom Ericsson*. Doktorsavhandling i teknikhistoria: KTH Arkitektur och samhällsbyggnad.

Meurling John & Jeans Richard (2000), *Den fula ankungen: hur Ericsson tog steget in i konsumentvarubranschen – med mobiltelefoner*. Ericsson Mobile Communications.

Nilsson, Agneta (2009), *En makalös förändring: Vattenfall 1985-2000*. Vattenfall.

Wood Donna J. (1991), Social issues in management: Theory and Research in Corporate Social Performance. *Journal of Management*, https://doi.org/10.1177%2F014920639101700206.

Thanks!

I would like to express my greatest gratitude to *the Karl Staaf Foundation*, which made this book possible by financing my project and the opportunity to print and publish the book. Thanks also to Arash and Martin who, during various periods, have been a sounding board regarding the meaning of CSR but also for their solid support regarding language and content. Finally, I would like to thank my family who have supported me when I have had to focus on this project!